New Law Practice

A New Lawyer's Guide

To

Starting & Building a New Law Practice

Economically!

D. CARR

Professional and Business Publishing

DEDICATION

Alice,

Here's to new beginnings!

Table of Contents

CHAPTER 1 - ENTREPRENEURSHIP **12**

DEFINITION **12**
THE QUESTIONS 14
THE ENTREPRENEURIAL MINDSET **18**
IT STARTS WITH A VISION 18
YOU ARE ON A MISSION..19
CREATIVE JUICES... 20
NO FAILURE, ONLY RESULTS...22
THE ENTREPRENEUR'S STRATEGY **25**
BE SELF-TAUGHT 25
BETTER, FASTER, MORE AFFORDABLE.............................27
LISTEN TO THE MARKET... 29

CHAPTER 2 - THE BASICS **31**

WHAT IS MY BUDGET? **31**
SOURCES FOR FUNDS...32
FAMILY AND FRIENDS 33
PRE-PAID LEGAL SERVICE 34
DISCOUNTED LEGAL SERVICES 35
POTENTIAL INVESTORS 36
IMMEDIATE CLIENTS 37
SAVINGS AND ASSETS YOU CAN SELL.............................38
OTHER EMPLOYMENT 39

BARTER OPPORTUNITIES 40
LOCATION, LOCATION, LOCATION...42
THE HOME OFFICE 44
THE VIRTUAL OFFICE 46
THE TRADITIONAL OFFICE..48
OFFICE LEASE 49
BUSINESS ENTITY..51
THE I.R.S..54
PHONE SERVICE 55
OCCUPATIONAL LICENSE 58
BUSINESS CARDS & STATIONERY..60
BUSINESS EQUIPMENT 63
BANK ACCOUNTS 67
ACCEPTING CREDIT AND DEBIT CARDS..70
ACCOUNTING SYSTEM 73
BUSINESS ATTIRE..76

CHAPTER 3 - FINDING NEW CLIENTS 80

MARKETING STRATEGY 84
MARKET RESEARCH 85
PRICING 97
ADVERTISING & MEDIA SELECTION 106

CHAPTER 4 - KEEPING CLIENTS AND BUILDING YOUR
PRACTICE 146

PRESENTATION & DELIVERY..147
OF SERVICE..147
PERSONAL 152
OFFICE..164
WORK..165
FOLLOW UP 167

CLIENT DATABASE 168
MARKETING CONSISTENCY 171
SURVEYS 173

FINAL WORD **174**

ABOUT THE AUTHOR **176**

INTRODUCTION

Congratulations!

Either, you just graduated law school, or have finally decided to go out on your own. Whatever the reason, congratulations are in order. New opportunities and options are right in front of you. This is a defining moment in your life. Ready or not, you are here.

Maybe you are finding yourself here, unexpectedly. The recent effects of the economic downturn, and a super saturation of new law school graduates caused a market phenomenon. Many law firms are not hiring as before. There seems to be more lawyers than lawyer job opportunities. Combine this with the large number of displaced lawyers that are still trying to stabilize their careers after the recession, with a new graduating class of new lawyers every year, and you understand the great competitive situation. I will bet that you never thought that a lawyer would be in this situation. The legal profession has held an almost sacred status, and always symbolized power, security, and prestige. It still does, but just like any other service offered for compensation, it must compete in the market place. Just like any other business, the law firm must compete for clients in order to survive.

The majority of you reading this book are not here because of your choice. I am sure that most of you would prefer to be securely employed in a large powerful law firm, enjoying a big salary. With so many law firms becoming lean, downsizing and closing, why would this be a good time to go solo? Stay hopeful! There are many reasons.

First, the larger firms have huge overhead and must downsize if the amount of business drops. As a solo firm, you do not, and can survive with a fraction of the amount of business. Remember, all your production is yours to manage. You do not need to share it with others.

Second, the law firms that are not run like a business fail just like any other poorly managed business. During the good times, there was plenty of business to be had. Law firms did not need to hunt for clients. Many never learned how. Now that times are tight, those who lack the knowledge and ability to see new opportunities and find new clients will find it very difficult to survive. You, as a new solo practitioner, are going out for your piece of the pie. You are educating yourself in the most important function of business: how to get clients. You are stepping away from the norm. Your chances for survival have just increased well beyond the average lawyer.

It feels a bit scary and exciting at the same time; doesn't it? I know. I have been there many times in my life. I assure you there is not a more rewarding experience than starting and building your own business. There are proven ways to succeed and to fail. The wheel does not have to be reinvented. Commit yourself to learning how to be an entrepreneur and a student of your own business.

From this day on, you are declaring your independence. You will be in complete control of how successful you will be, and how long it will take you to get there. No one but you will decide your worth or quality of life. Work will be more fulfilling because the rewards are all yours.

Let's begin…

Chapter 1 -
Entrepreneurship

Definition

My definition of Entrepreneurship is the creation or management of any business, guided by unwavering initiative and passion, and involving great determination and management of risk.

To be an entrepreneur, one must adopt certain traits and think a certain way. It is a level of awareness, motivation, and thought about creating and operating a business of your own, your way!

Many universities and graduate schools attempt to teach entrepreneurship. Many of them even have a curriculum to follow. The entrepreneurship programs I have examined are no more than a collection of business management courses. Studying business management, although helpful in learning business theory, does not make you an entrepreneur. Entrepreneurship is not a degree, but more of an attitude and desire.

If entrepreneurship sounds philosophical to you, it is because it is a belief, more so than it is knowledge. Feel good about this! It is not another school course or complicated material that you will have to force yourself to learn. It is more of a realization or clarification of an awakened desire to create and nurture something that will provide emotional and financial satisfaction.

How can entrepreneurship be truly learned in its most pure form? The lesson begins with a series of very personal questions to ask of yourself. The answers are different for everyone. They are different because the questions mean something different to everyone. They require that you search deep for your own personal needs, purpose, reasons, and motivation. The answers will have a profound meaning to you, and you alone. By starting your personal quest for answers, you will start to see and feel the right path to becoming a true entrepreneur, in every sense of the word.

The Questions

A. *Why do you want to start a law practice of your own?*

Maybe it is because you can't find a job, or are about to lose one. Maybe it is because you desire more freedom to work the way you want, instead of being told what assignments you are allowed to work on. Perhaps it is because you want more control and a better balance between work and life. Whatever the reason, it is a good reason, because it is yours! Whether your reason(s) are out of necessity or by choice, it doesn't matter. Motivation is motivation, no matter the source of inspiration.

B. *Do you have what it takes to start a Solo Practice?*

Of course, you do! Don't be afraid of the question. The meaning of the question is, "Do you want to start a Solo Practice?" We all have what it takes. All that is required is determination and the willingness to learn. You don't need any more training to be a lawyer. The state Bar that admitted you says that you are a lawyer. The rest is business strategy, which we will discuss later in the book.

C. *Does the idea of owning your own law practice excite you?*

If you feel butterflies in your stomach, or some fear and curiosity of the unknown, the answer is yes. Just the fact that you are reading this book affirms this. All you need at this stage is a bit of curiosity, fear, and maybe excitement. The best thing that follows is more excitement, as you start to see results that "you" created from nothing but an idea and desire.

D. *Are you willing to learn how to start your own law practice, and more importantly, continue learning and improving your entrepreneurial skills?*

This question is very important. What distinguishes a true entrepreneur from the average businessperson is the burning desire to keep learning and improving. Think about it. When your law practice starts to fulfill your needs, and shows great promise to provide you with a great life, pride, and security, why wouldn't you want to nurture it and make it everything you dreamed it could be?

E. *Can you visualize yourself in your own firm, doing things "your way"?*

Go ahead. Dream a little. How do you look? What does your office look like? Are you as busy as you want to be? What cases are you working on? Has your family seen your office? Are they proud? Aren't you proud of your accomplishments? Do you see how much your clients need and trust you? Do you feel passionate about the important work you chose to work on? Doesn't it feel good to be the best lawyer in town? Doesn't it feel good that everyone knows it? Doesn't it feel good not to have to worry about money, because you are making what you want? How does it feel to be your own boss?

F. What does it mean to you to be successful?

Success is something different to everyone. My definition of success is when you accomplish the lifestyle that provides you with meaningful experiences, security, and opportunities for growth by doing what you want and enjoy. Success could be the end result or the journey to it, or both! Only you can define what makes you feel successful. Somebody else's definition won't work. Many people trap themselves in the wrong path or result by following someone else's definition of success, and not their own. Just know that you don't have to have it all mapped out right now. The fun part is that you can redefine your success anytime and as many times as you see fit. It is your life and your own happiness.

The exercise you just completed started the process that will help clarify your business goal. Keep these images in mind as you read on. Write down the answers to the questions in a private place. You can refer to them as you expand your thoughts, or change your answers. Remember, you are not bound to keep your plans unchanged. Fine tune them or change them as often as you wish. These are "your" rules and "your" strategies. No one will criticize or judge but you. As you read on, feel free to write down ideas that inspire you. These notes and ideas are like fuel to the entrepreneur.

The entrepreneurial mindset

It starts with a vision

Dreaming in business is a powerful tool. Dreaming is visualizing. Any great plan or business starts with a vision. The beauty of dreaming is that there are no physical limitations. You are free to visualize yourself doing anything. It is true creative freedom. The more you visualize the more clear the way to your goal will become.

Start with an image. Your answers to the questions in the previous section would be a good place to start. Continue to picture these images, and then start to wonder how you can actualize them. What are the obstacles? What are the possibilities? Write notes as you imagine good ideas. Expand them with short plans of action. Pretty soon, a more complete plan will appear.

A small notepad that fits in your pocket will come in handy when ideas pop in your head. The mind is a creative engine that constantly works, even when you are not aware of it. Allow for this type of creativity. By keeping images of questions or what you want to occur in your thoughts throughout the day, your mind will work at ways to realize them. Have you ever had an idea or a solution come to you, out of the blue? This is your subconscious mind at work. You were probably wondering about a question or problem and didn't realize that your mind continues to "wander," even when you consciously stop.

Successful entrepreneurs dream and visualize their desired goal in business. You are now creating the foundation of the entrepreneurial mindset. It is what should be in your head constantly, when planning and running your law practice. It is the mental "carrot" in front of you, guiding and prioritizing all your business efforts to keep you focused on the prize: a successful law practice.

You are on a mission

Determination and passion drives the entrepreneur. You obtained this book because you want to start your own successful law firm. You have the need and the desire. Who or what is standing in your way, preventing you from realizing this vision? How bad do you want it? Enough to allow yourself the opportunity to accomplish it? Enough to figure out a way around any obstacle? Enough, to want to learn everything you can to ensure your success? It is not enough to just say, "I'll try." You must be on a sacred mission to make it happen for yourself, and you must commit yourself to it. A wise mentor once told me a powerful statement, "If it's to be, it's up to me." Ponder the thought. Who else is going to make things happen for you, but you? Who else knows your true needs and desires that make you happy, but you? Get the point? Get started, continue, and do not stop. It's your life and livelihood. Do all it requires of you to achieve your goal. Learn everything you need to allow yourself to master what you need to succeed.

Creative juices...

Creativity is the business license of the entrepreneur. It is what makes you invincible. There is no business puzzle that can't be solved. Creativity does not recognize physical limitations or obstacles. It is not bound by it. It is free-flowing. It feeds on itself.

Have you ever felt butterflies in your stomach? It is a feeling of excitement and anxiety of what's to come... known or unknown. Remember wondering about the possibilities, and getting more excited? This is what I mean about creativity feeding on itself. It is fuel for thought. The mind races with possibilities. The feeling is very real, as if you were actually experiencing it.

So, how could this process be consciously initiated? If you remember, it started with a desire, an exciting desire. Make a mental note if you felt excited during the visualization exercise. If you did not, dig deeper. Look for something that doesn't just provide basic needs. Look for the "want" factor. Sure, a successful law firm will pay the bills, feed you, and clothe you. But, what else do you want? What excites you about the possibility of being your own boss, with no one to report to?

Finding what excites you about running your own law practice won't be difficult. It will take a little more dreaming. Imagine it so that you can believe it. Visualize until you can feel the enjoyment. Maybe it is the complete control of your time and the quality of the free time it creates. Maybe it is the car you see yourself driving. Or, the house or apartment you see yourself living in. Perhaps it's the prestige or image you want to project, or the level of competence you seek. Or, the social circle you see yourself in. Whatever the image, use it to fuel your excitement, as you begin taking steps to make the image true.

This excitement will start and keep you dreaming and wondering, and will allow you to piece it all together, like a puzzle you are solving. Your goals and desires are your puzzle. There is not only one way to solve the puzzle; there are as many solutions as you can invent. Allow yourself the creative freedom to explore any and all possibilities.

No failure, only results...

Believe it, because it is your secret super power. The thought is very powerful. It means that you cannot fail. Imagine everything you could do, and "would do," if there was no way to fail. Limitless possibilities, right? Fear may be a factor, but not a limiting factor, because you were guaranteed not to fail. The challenge would be interesting, wouldn't it?

Let's examine the concept of failure. The definition is, "lack of success." It means not getting the desired results that you set out to get. The fear of the concept of failure is your perception of how you think others will see your failure, and how it will affect your own self-perception or self-esteem and confidence. It brings about shame from not achieving what was promised. The shame or even the fear of shame can cripple you. The fear of failure can keep you from trying. It plays with the mind by trying to protect you from the pain, fear, and shame of failing. It will kill your creativity. It will prevent you from your great potential.

The key to understanding failure is to dissect the definition. First, failure means lack of success. Remember that you are the only one defining the meaning of success for yourself, no one else! You will not create mental fences around your possibilities. Mental fences take many shapes:

- Time Schedules
- Unrealistic Expectations
- Broken Promises to Others
- Promises Made to Yourself and Others
- Trying to Fulfill Others' Dreams for You

When you decide to take action, do not set yourself up for disappointment. Understand that you are trying out an idea, not an end all plan. Whatever results you get are good results, because they give you a better and truer understanding of the task at hand. With any result you get one step closer, because you are eliminating ineffective actions and implementing effective ones. This is your experiment, no one else's.

The second key to understanding failure is the fear, through the perception others form of your perceived failure. Why is anyone else in the position to judge you? They shouldn't be. The answer to this is very simple; don't share your experiments with anyone! Your decisions are for no one to judge but you. And, even if you are the judge, don't beat yourself up. Look at it like a game, a very fun game that only you play. The prize, if you win, is huge. Only you have the opportunity to play and you will not compete for the prize. You get as many chances to win, as you like. Keep playing until you win the big prize. No hurry, no clock, no deadline, no judges! Just you and your eye on the prize! Start again as many times as you wish.

The entrepreneur's strategy

Be Self-Taught

You are the only one who can facilitate or limit your chances for business success. Knowledge is power. It has always been, and will always be. How much business knowledge you learn is up to you. To master anything, one must continue to learn. This is true for you, as a businessperson, and as an attorney. For the same reasons why you must have continuing education to maintain your license, you must continue learning how you can be more effective, in order to stay in business.

To be self-taught, you must be aware of anything that can make you a better attorney and business owner. You must be willing to continuously improve, change, or modify what could be better. This is done by being observant. Observe and be aware of how your efforts affect you and your clients. Compare your efforts and strategies with other businesses, not just other lawyers. Notice the little things that leave big impressions on you as a consumer and customer. Listen to the comments or opinions others make about their experience with any business.

We are all very similar when it comes to judging an experience with an individual or business organization. Our impressions of an experience are positive or negative, strong or weak, trusting or doubtful, friendly or casual, believable or not, pleasant or cold, etc. Get the idea? These impressions decide if we continue a relationship, trust it to try again, pay more for it, or eliminate it as a choice.

Be aware and take note of your experiences. Identify what gave you that perception or feeling. Adapt your business efforts to either include or eliminate these strategies that may affect your business and client perceptions.

Sources for this type of knowledge are your own personal experiences and other people's opinions. Other people's opinions can easily be found in different ways. One way is to simply ask. Another way is to look for customer comments and complaints. They can be found in many online business directories, where a customer may leave comments. Study these carefully. You will notice that we all have basic expectations and expect them to be met in any business transaction. Sometimes promises are made by the business, in the form of advertising messages or images shown. Customers may comment on their satisfaction or disappointment with how their expectations were met. There is a good business saying, "under-promise and over-deliver." What counts to a customer or client is not whether you sold them to do business with you, but whether you earned their business and can keep them coming back for more!

Remember, as a professional and business organization, one can always improve. Take this to heart or you will fade away. The market is too competitive to just stay compliant. A successful business must continue to improve.

Better, Faster, More Affordable

Think of all the products or services that are now out of business. I guarantee you that it was because another service or product did the same job better, faster, and is more affordable. Here are some examples:

- Video Rental Stores - replaced by mini rental boxes at convenience stores and supermarkets. These kiosks more conveniently offered the same movie for less. Online streaming or downloading have now replaced these. Better, faster, more affordable.
- Cable TV and Satellite TV - expensive services are being replaced by off air digital antenna and the

Internet. You can watch anything at any time, either for free or less expensive. Better, faster, more affordable.

- Specialty Stores - replaced by mega department stores. And now, the mega stores are being replaced by online stores. Buy anything in one convenient place. Better, faster, more affordable.
- Full Service Law Firms - currently being replaced by small boutique firms that are more specialized, and have less overhead and red tape. Better, faster, more affordable.

There are many more examples. The market conditions are changing all the time. New businesses are opening offering better, faster, and more affordable services and products. Old business models unwilling to improve, adapt, or change go out of business daily. The current economy speeds up the process by demanding better, faster, and more affordable products and services. New customers and clients will choose whom they do business with and how much they will pay, by this expectation.

Now, you have heard the following defensive statements:

- Cheaper is not always better.
- You get what you pay for.

- You must pay more for quality.

Never repeat these to a prospective client! Why, you ask? It is because you and the client know they are false. The customer knows them to be a sales pitch to get them to pay more, especially "before" they have experienced the service or product. These statements should be realizations that your client makes "after" they have experienced your services, and not as a pre-warning that they are about to pay more.

Listen to the market...

Many businesses operate in the dark by constantly offering products and services, without researching if the customer even wants or needs them. They put the cart before the horse. These businesses do not last too long and close up eventually, when the money runs out. You can see examples of these businesses all the time. Just walk through a mall or shopping strip. They started as a hopeful idea and not as a response to what the market is calling for.

Another crazy example is a business that repeats the same mistake as a recently failed one. How many times do you see a recently closed restaurant replaced by another restaurant in the same location, sometimes even serving a similar menu? Crazy! The market is clearly and loudly saying, "No!"

To have a successful business, you must give the customer what it wants. So what does the customer want from your new law practice? It depends on many factors:

- Who are your prospective clients?
- Where is your office located?
- What is the current economic condition?
- Who is your competitor?
- How do your services compare?
- Are you ready, willing, and able to make your services, you guessed it, better, faster, and more affordable?

Chapter 2 - The Basics

What is my budget?

The first consideration in starting your practice is deciding what your budget is. In order to plan a budget, you'll need to know how much money you have to work with. If you are just out of law school, and do not have much or any, it's OK. We will just need to be creative and frugal. It can still be done. If you have access to funds, then you will start out ahead of everyone else who does not. From this point, we will discuss options and solutions as if you were limited with funds. If you are, read on. You may learn other solutions to add to your resources and expand your options.

Let's examine some possibilities. If you do not have funds set aside to start your practice and maintain the doors open, do you have access to some? Think of all possible sources and make a list. Next, structure a realistic working budget as we continue. We will be discussing all the necessary steps to get your practice started. As you read on, take notes of the minimum necessities and calculate the cost. You are going to be amazed at how much of what you need is already in your possession.

Ideally, you would want just the necessary expenses to last you a year. Now, let's take a look at where you can find these funds.

Sources for Funds

- Family
- Friends
- Potential Investors
- Immediate Clients
- Savings
- Assets you can sell
- Other Employment
- Barter Opportunities

Family and Friends

Family and friends are a great source of funding. You would be surprised at how supportive and willing they already are. If you just graduated law school, your family and friends must be very proud. Are you the first in your family or among your friends to accomplish such an important professional degree? Are you the only lawyer in your family? Do you know a family member or friend who is currently in need of legal help?

You know everyone is proud of your accomplishment. They must not only be proud but also excited to have a lawyer in the family, or to be friends with one! Many of them would be happy to help you get started. You just need to ask. Don't be shy. You won't be asking for a free handout. You will be offering them a valuable opportunity.

Everyone experiences a time when they need a lawyer. Having your own personal lawyer, ready, willing, and able to step in front and protect your rights, is invaluable. It is important insurance for life's unexpected and expected challenges. And, if your lawyer is your family or your friend... even better! It is prestigious.

Before you rush out to ask your family and friends for funds, think of a proposal that provides a valuable exchange for their investment. Here are some ideas:

Pre-Paid Legal Service

Put together several options and levels of rewards for different amounts of investment. Research how much a lawyer's hour is worth in your area. It will probably vary by experience and area of law. It would probably fall in the range between $250 and $350 per hour. Offer them double the value for their investment. For example, a $500 investment would guarantee those 4 hours of legal services or $1,000 towards any flat fee service (based on $250 per hour). Offer different options to make it affordable, such as $250, $500, $750, etc. They could secure the use of this reduced pre-paid legal fee, and use it any time within 2 years. Add the option that you will honor the use toward their immediate family's future legal needs, and it is quite an opportunity. Most will help you anyway, but it sweetens the opportunity because they are receiving something of value in return: access to their lawyer!

Discounted Legal Services

Who, among your family and friends, are in immediate need of legal help and can benefit from your professional services, at a "family and friends discount rate?" Research lawyers' fees for the following:

- Last Will and Testament
- Living Will
- Designation of Medical Surrogate
- Power of Attorney
- Attorney Letter
- Contract for Purchase or Sale
- Quit Claim Deeds
- Mortgage and Note
- Lease Agreement
- Bankruptcy
- Foreclosure Defense
- Uncontested Divorce (amicable and civil)
- DUI Defense
- Other services that may be needed

After you research what other lawyers are charging for the above, offer a "family discount" or a "special discount" of maybe 25% or 30% off your normal price (market price). Be sure to show your normal price on their invoice or statement, and also show the amount of discount they are receiving.

Potential Investors

Anyone can be a potential investor. Investors invest. They give you funds with an expectation of a return on their invested money. In other words, they loan you money. Structure an agreement in which you promise them a fair and competitive rate of return. Research banks, finance companies, and credit unions. Quote a return slightly above their loan interest rates. Depending on the economic market, these may be low or high. Remember that you will be paying these loans back with interest, so be realistic.

Be a lawyer in your own negotiations and create a favorable situation for yourself. Maybe your investment agreement can state that you secure the amount borrowed with a guaranteed amount of legal work. Say, valued at one and a half (1.5) times the amount borrowed.

Example: you borrow $10,000 to be paid back in 5 years, at 10% annual rate of return ($1,000 interest per year). No payments due for 12 months, guaranteed by $15,000 in legal work to be used within 2 years. This is just an example. You can structure it any way that you and your investor find agreeable. Seek the advice of someone who knows more about this, like your banker, parents, accountant, etc. You want to leave investors as your last resort. You want to avoid any type of debt that does not directly produce income for you.

Notice we have not discussed the use of loans or credit cards. The only type of leveraging you should consider are investors and only under the structure I described above. By securing their investment with an amount of legal work equal to a greater rate of return, you would only owe services and not money if you were not able to pay off the investment. Using credit cards or loans to fund your business venture is a great gamble, especially for a new professional. You risk damaging your credit or license if you cannot make your payments. It's not worth it. Credit should only be used as a calculated risk in which you are sure of the expectations of earnings.

Immediate Clients

Let's wait a little while for this topic. It deserves a chapter on the topic of how to obtain immediate clients. We will be discussing how to find immediate clients later in the book.

Savings and Assets You Can Sell

Think of what you may own that has value. I do not mean lawyer services, but actual property. Online sites that allow you to list stuff for sale can help you raise some funds. Some of these are:

- eBay
- Craigslist
- Amazon

Search your home for your stuff, and ask others (family and friends) to donate unwanted stuff and offer to pick it up. Schedule a garage sale and list the items on sites like the above. Here are some ideas for items that may have value to others:

- Bicycles
- Tools
- Yard Equipment
- Yard Furniture
- CDs
- Clothing
- Furniture
- Electronics
- Collections
- Vehicles

- Sunglasses
- Cell Phones
- Etc., etc., etc.

You get the idea.

Other Employment

Here is where you remember past times in which you thought like an entrepreneur. As a kid, maybe you mowed the neighbor's lawn, painted, cleaned, tutored, etc. Make a list of what you can do and call everyone. You now have a great story! You are working to save enough to open your law firm. I cannot imagine anyone who wouldn't think or say, "Wow."

Tell them that you will remember them when you are established as the ones who helped you get started. What a compliment, and what a great cause to give you work. You may not need much to get started, and you may have raised a lot already with the other methods discussed earlier. You may just need a few small jobs to get you to your goal.

Nurture these jobs, and schedule them as an ongoing, great source of flexible work to create much needed income until your practice picks up. It won't be long until $250 an hour starts adding up and you won't need the small jobs.

Here are some ideas for flexible work:
- Mow Lawns

- Do Yard Work & Clean Up Yards
- Clean Garage or Organize (for stuff to sell)
- Wash and Detail Cars
- Help with Moving
- Painting (sheds, houses, fences, rooms, etc.)
- Steam Clean Carpet (rent equipment)
- Gardening
- Tutoring Services (advertise individually & with schools)
- Freelance Paralegal (for other lawyers)
- Etc., etc., etc.

Barter Opportunities

Bartering is just trading one thing of value for another, instead of paying with cash. In tight economic times, more people are using property and services as currency. Look online for Bartering listings. Get creative. You need a lot of stuff to get started that you can trade for your unwanted stuff or services, even legal work (we'll discuss more later). Here is a list of things you may be able to Barter for:

- Advertising
- Office Space
- Copier

- Computer
- Cell Phone
- Secretarial Services
- Stationery (custom envelopes, business cards, etc.)
- Anything!

So, did you find funds that you did not think you had? Surprised? You just completed an interesting exercise. You used your creativity, gathered your resources, and made something happen! This way of thinking is exactly what you need to succeed in business. As you read on, take notes on the Bare necessities and keep a running total. Towards the end of the book, we will use that amount as a guide to plan a budget.

Location, Location, Location...

The second consideration in starting your practice is its location. Your office address is very important. To the client, it expresses an image about you, your success and your competence. You will be competing for clients with every other attorney in business. The client's impression of you is very important. Everything you express about yourself should say, "I am a professional," "I am successful," and "You can trust me."

Of course, we have to be realistic about the budget. However, this does not mean that we have to be limited by it. Remember, the image is a perception, not reality. Think of what a fine tailored suit says to everyone about who is wearing it. Everyone may not know it's your only suit. Or what a professionally designed website says about the company it's about, even if the company is small. Some creativity and business sense will take you very far. We will discuss different office structures, starting from a home office to a plush downtown set up.

The most important factors when choosing the location of your office are:

- Is it easy for your clients to find you
- Is parking easily available
- Does the location make a statement (professionalism, successful, trustworthy)
- Is it centrally located (access to clients all around you)
- Is it within a short drive to the courts where you will be practicing
- Are there other professionals in the building or nearby (networking, referrals, mentoring, etc.)
- Is it affordable (within your budget)

For now, narrow it down to the area. Think of the type of law you want to practice. The type of law will help you develop a client profile and location. For example:

- Estate Planning
  - Established Neighborhoods
  - Senior Centers
  - Nursing Homes
- Family Law
  - Anywhere
- Landlord Tenant Law
  - Affordable Neighborhoods (Rentals)

o   Apartment Complexes

You get the idea. If you do not want to narrow your choices right now, and want to get a feel for the market demand, stay central. This is a good idea if you are starting a new practice. Business is all about filling a need in your market. Stay open and be quick to respond to the demand message that the market is giving.

The Home Office

Working from home may be the right choice to start out. However, it is not the place to meet with clients. It is only where you work. If you just graduated law school and are living at home as a way to minimize business and living expenses, that is great! This is one of your resources that we spoke about, and you are fortunate to have it.

A home office has many advantages. A dining room is rarely used and is a perfect desk. Files can be kept in your room or closet. Make sure you check with your State Bar as to the requirements of where you store client files. Privacy rules may require you to put a lock on your room door. This is very easy and inexpensive. Your local hardware should sell lock handles for as little as $12. Maybe you already have a laptop and printer that you used to do your law schoolwork. An all-in-one printer is ideal (prints, scans, faxes, copies). You can use your local office supply store for supplies, copies, faxes, scans, etc. The internet service in your home will be very useful. If you don't have internet, check the wireless networks reaching your home. Maybe a neighbor would let you pay a fraction of their bill for you to access their internet. Better yet, maybe you can Barter!

Remember, a home office is perfect to start out, but you don't want to meet with clients at your home. It will give a weak impression. It is just not professional. So where can you meet with clients? Think of the marketing advantage of this situation. You can go to them. A lawyer that makes house calls! That is a way to set you apart from the crowd. Of course, you won't be able to continue this when you get busy, but what a great way to get there. This is the best part... Clients will pay you extra for the convenience!

Meeting clients at their home offers other fringe benefits. It is a more relaxed environment. The client is comfortable and will be more concerned about making you feel comfortable, instead of the other way around. You will be treated like a guest. You can build rapport and break the ice quicker. This will work for you, being new to dealing with clients. When you get busy and have business meetings at your office, you can use the same skills in helping the client feel comfortable with you. The best benefit of all is that you just got a head start to building a friendship. You were at their home! Nurture this. Friends are clients forever!

The Virtual Office

The virtual office is a terrific concept that started some years ago. If you are working from home, consider combining it with a virtual office. For a fraction of the price to have your own office, you can have all the advantages and benefits of having an office of your own. For a very low monthly fee, you can have access to a posh office, when you need it. These are very popular downtown. They are perfect for lawyers, especially if you are just starting out.

The virtual office is usually a group of offices, in a professional office building. They are managed by a company that specializes in office support services. The company sets up the office space with:

- Furnished offices
- Conference or meeting rooms
- Lobby or waiting area
- Receptionist to answer phones and greet clients

- Secretarial services available when you need it
- Office equipment (computer, copier, fax, printer, etc.)
- Internet and phone
- Mail service
- Phone answering service
- Included amount of office and meeting room time

The virtual offices that I researched ranged in price from $150 to $250 per month. They include 10 to 15 hours of office and meeting room time, with additional time available to rent at $15 to $20 an hour. It is the perfect amount of time to meet 10 to 15 clients per month for an hour each. They vary from modest professional offices in easy to reach commercial office parks to very posh and high-end offices in downtown high-rise office buildings. They have a professional appearance and would enhance your professional message to your client.

Normally, a setup of your own to match the look and conveniences of a virtual office would run you many thousands of dollars in initial investment plus a few thousand dollars per month in rent and services, not including the support staff. The benefits are outstanding:

- Image of being established
- Message of success, professionalism and trust

- Usually, many locations you can use

- A real address to advertise and receive mail

- A receptionist to greet clients

- Modern and luxurious furnishings and facility

- Secretarial services when you need it

- Internet access

- Phone service, if you need it

The Traditional Office

We won't be covering a traditional office for the purposes of this book. It would require a yearly lease term, as well as the extra cost to furnish and equip with all the necessary tools. It would also require a receptionist, or your office would be closed when you are in court or in the field. I would not recommend it for a new lawyer just starting out. There are other good options, as discussed earlier, without the gamble and long-term commitment.

Office Lease

Long-term commitments are not recommended to start out. It is too risky and a huge gamble to commit yourself, your new practice, your credit, and your good reputation on an unknown bet. Leave yourself as many options as possible until you get better established. Right now, you do not know how quickly your practice will grow. You might outgrow your choice of office and will have to wait until the lease is over to move. On the other hand, you might lock yourself into an office that is too much, too soon, and be stuck paying for unused space.

This is why I am very partial to the Virtual Office. Usually, the terms are very flexible, often leased on a month-to-month basis. This gives you all kinds of options:

- Move out anytime with just a 30 days' notice.
- Start out with an affordable plan and add services as needed.
- Only pay for what you need.
- No long-term commitment.
- No upfront deposits.
- No utility costs.
- No long term staffing costs.

When comparing the office setup, consider the lease terms carefully. If you found a nice professional office, don't be bashful, negotiate the lease!

Business Entity

The third consideration in starting your practice is what business entity to operate under. By business entity, I mean legal structure such as corporation or sole proprietor. There are other types of business entities like LLC, partnerships, etc. However, assuming that you are going solo, an S corporation or sole proprietorship are good options to start.

The preferable choice, in my opinion, is to operate as a corporation. From your studies, you know that a sole proprietorship is no different than working under your own name. You would also be completely open to all kinds of liability. The corporate structure provides many benefits:

- A shield for your personal assets against business liability. This is not so much for attorneys because it is your own services that you will be selling, and therefore you would be responsible for any damage caused to a client or the public.

- Separate business structure to separate your personal affairs from your business operation.

- Easier accounting of business. Avoid co-mingling your personal funds with your business capital.

- Well-structured tax rules and tax allowances. Banks love the corporate structure when it comes to lending or leasing for your future needs. Unlike a self-employed person (sole proprietor), a corporate employee implies more stability.

- Most states offer a special designation for business professionals like attorneys, CPA's, architects, etc. This designation is "P.A." or Professional Association.

Check with the Secretary of State's website for corporation start up information. You should be able to do it all online. First, think of a name for your business. A common choice for most solos is, "Law Office of (your name), P.A." Once you decide on your business name, go online to your state's website and file your Articles of Incorporation. This is the form that establishes the registration of your new corporation. Every year after, you would need to file an "Annual Report" on the same website. This basically lets everyone know your corporation is still in business. Remember from your studies that a business corporation needs to have annual meetings and minutes of those meetings. Yes, even your one-man corporation. Revisit those Business Law notes.

I know that there may be reasons to choose other business entities. You are a lawyer! If you have a better choice, execute it. My purpose for this book is to get right down to what I consider to be the simplest and most economical choice. By all means, research for yourself. You may agree with my advice.

One great benefit to a corporation structure is that all earnings the business makes are the business' income, not yours, as long as you do not write yourself a paycheck! How is this beneficial to you? I assume that you may have some student loans? Yes? Maybe, you are trying to negotiate a payment deferment or payment plan based on income. Well, there you go. You do not have an income, as long as your business is not paying you. This can buy you more time to get established and more prepared before you start making your student loan payments. This can be done for the entire year until tax time in January. Consult with your accountant (a great opportunity to establish a relationship with a fellow professional).

The I.R.S.

Ha-ha... Don't fret. This will be a pleasant call. You are going to ask the I.R.S. how to pay your taxes.

Go to www.irs.gov. There you will search for two things. First, is "how to apply for a FEIN." As your Federal Employer Identification Number, this is basically your new business's tax ID. It is how the I.R.S. will recognize your business tax account. Second, you need to search for "how to request an S-Corporation status." An S-Corp. is a wonderful designation that the I.R.S. grants some small businesses. Again, open up your Tax Law notes. A regular corporation or C-Corp. is subject to potential double taxation. This means that the corporation pays income tax on its earnings and you pay again when you receive your employee earnings. An S-Corp's earnings flow straight to you, the Director or Officer of your corporation. You bypass the corporate level of taxation.

Phone Service

A cellular phone is definitely the best way to start. Compare service plans. If you are not part of your parents' service plan, consider it. Usually, it would only cost an extra $10 or $20 to add another line to an existing plan. Ideally, you would need the following:

- Voice mail with professional message (Pleasant professional voice, preferably female, but not your own).

- A service plan with unlimited minutes.

- An easy to remember phone number (the service provider can find you a repetitive number. You could change your present one for about $10 to $20).

- Voice recorder feature to record notes or meetings authorized to be recorded.

- A camera with decent resolution (3 mega-pixel or better). This makes for a handy copier and scanner.

- Internet and Email capability is nice, but not crucial. Presently, Wi-Fi is available in most restaurants, bookstores, coffee shops, etc., so you can connect on your laptop when you need to.

- Earpiece for hands-free talks.
- Mute feature. This is your "hold" button.
- Conference Call Feature
- Caller ID

Most of these features are already included at no extra charge, or at minimal cost. This will be your office line. You will have immediate access wherever you are, so you'll never miss a client's call. Put all your friends and family in the phone's memory, so you can identify them with the caller ID. Ask the service provider to correct the outgoing caller ID to show "Law Office" or "Your Name." Every other call should be answered, "Good Morning (or afternoon), Law Office of 'Your Name.' This is 'You,' how may I help you?" Smile; the way you answer your business line reflects your attitude and tone to the person at the other end!

Another type of phone service that you need is a fax number. It is not necessary for you to subscribe to a landline or purchase a fax machine. There are several online services that provide online fax service. They give you a dedicated fax number that is your own. This is great because the faxes are sent as attachments to an email that you could receive anywhere. You could also just print the ones you need and delete or store the rest. You also have the ability to send faxes through the service website or your email account. You would basically scan the document to be faxed and attach the PDF file. The monthly subscription fees vary between $7 and $12 per month. It is very affordable. As a solo practitioner, the mobility feature is priceless. Some cell phones can also receive faxes. Faxing may seem antiquated, but you will be surprised how often it is still used. Check with your cell phone service provider.

Occupational License

Most cities and counties have adopted an alternate name for the occupational license. The new term is "Business Tax Receipt." It is the same thing. You might need various Occupational Licenses; one from the state, county, and city. The state license is your Bar number. You will obtain this number when you pass your state BAR exam. The county and city licenses depend on where your office is located. If your office is situated within the city boundaries, then you will need both a city and county license. If the office is outside city limits, and within the county boundaries, then you will need a county license.

Call your city and county occupational license department to see which you need. The cost for the city and county license is minimal. Typically, these will range between $50 and a few hundred dollars. They are necessary and should be renewed annually.

Before you sign any office agreement or lease, check with the appropriate municipality to make sure that a law firm is allowed to operate there. If so, go ahead and secure the office space. You will need the address for the city and county license, as well as for the next topics (business cards, stationery, website, etc.). You will also need to inform the BAR of your new address.

Business Cards & Stationery

The business card will be one of your marketing tools. Give careful consideration to every detail. The message here should express "professional." Stay away from cute designs or wild fonts or graphics. A lawyer's business card should be very conservative, simple, serious, and elegant. Based on my experience, small print shops will be your best source for business cards. Large office supply chains have a more cookie- cutter approach and will not let you customize as much without an extra cost.

When you find a small print shop, call and ask if they cater to the legal professional. Ask to see samples of business cards for attorneys. Be aware of your first impression. Ask the printer which style and design is most elegant, simple, conservative, and serious. These are the attributes that potential clients will be drawn to.

A perfect lawyer business card, in my opinion, is one printed on card stock that resembles linen or parchment paper. The card stock is textured and not flimsy. The ink is black and raised. A simple elegant logo is appropriate. It contains just the necessary information:

- Your name
- Firm's name
- Address, City, State, Zip
- Office phone number
- Office fax number
- Email address
- Website address
- No additional marketing message of any kind

Order 1,000 in quantity. The price difference is not much from 500 or 250. You will use these in our marketing efforts, discussed later in the book.

Your office stationery should not be preprinted. I recommend the office supply store for these. Look for a parchment or linen paper that is similar to your business card. The paper should be slightly and noticeably heavier than standard copy paper. Buy matching envelopes. Design your letterhead to be similar to your business card and save it on your word processing program under "letterhead." When you type out a letter, your printer will print it on your letterhead at the same time. You could even print out envelopes for that professional look. This works best and it is much more economical than buying custom letterhead and envelopes.

Here is a helpful tip about the proper use of your professional stationery. In your practice you will be producing many letters, pleadings, briefs, etc. Use the fancy paper only for writing to your clients! It reflects on your work and will enhance its presentation and delivery. There is something about opening a letter from your attorney that feels prestigious, firm, serious, and professional. It creates an image about you and your firm.

Use the regular copy paper for everything else:

- Court Pleadings and Forms
- Correspondence with other attorneys
- Correspondence with vendors and suppliers
- Copies for your files
- Etc.

Business Equipment

The idea here is to use what you have. Avoid buying any equipment for now. It is an extra expense that you don't need, unless it is absolutely necessary. By absolutely necessary, I mean that you don't have access to equipment through copy centers, office supply stores, libraries, etc.

Let's examine the different business equipment and possible sources:

- **All-In-One** (printer, copier, scanner) – Most purchased printers have these features. The one that you used in law school should be perfect. A laser or toner output is more efficient, faster, and looks great. An inkjet printer has the same finished product appearance but will cost more to operate. The ink cartridges are for low quantity production. Laser printers are so inexpensive nowadays that it may make sense to buy one if you don't have one. Don't throw away your inkjet yet. The inkjet printer will print on the fancy paper stationery and envelopes better than the toner printer. Experiment with your letterhead on the fancy stationery and standard copy paper. If you can't put out the money right now, don't worry. The local copy center will have access to great copiers, fax service, and scanning of documents for a low usage fee. This way you just pay as you need, until you can buy an all-in-one.

- **Laptop Computer** – Your old school laptop will work great. There is no need to go out and buy a different laptop. The main software that you will use is simply a word processor and spreadsheet. You should already have these, but if not, there are plenty of free software versions online. Find one that can read or save documents in the same formats as popular office software. You will need Wi-Fi capability, which you probably already have, to access the internet mainly for email and research. If you still have a desktop computer, it's OK. It will still work great. You just won't be able to take it with you. Great sources for computer access are libraries, copy centers, internet cafés, and even your client's home, if you are making a house visit.

- **<u>Filing Cabinet</u>** – A small 2-drawer filing cabinet is sufficient to start out. It can easily fit under a worktable, desk, or closet. Check out your local office supply store for options. The cabinet should be metal and have a lock (unless it will be in a room that can be locked). It should be able to accommodate hanging folders on the top and bottom drawer. The size of the hanging folders could be letter size. Most legal documents fit this style or could easily be folded to size. Before buying a new cabinet, check online classifieds to see if you can find one at a Bargain. A pre-owned filing cabinet is just as functional as a new one.

- **<u>Office Supplies</u>** – You will need some basic office supplies. Shop around for the best prices and don't go overboard. Buy only what you need for a few months. Here is a list of the basic necessities:
  - Hanging Folders
  - Plain Manila Folders – Letter Size
  - 2 Prong Clasp Set – Client Files

- 2-Hole Punch
- Stapler, Staples, & Staple Remover
- Tape and Dispenser
- Paper Clips – Large and Small
- Yellow Stick-On – Note Pads
- Envelopes - #10 Plain White
- Copy Paper – Plain White
- Pens – Plain Stick Pens (blue, black, red)
- Highlighter – Yellow, Green, Pink
- White Out – Liquid
- Page Tabs – Stick on for client file
- Desktop Name Plate – (eg. Wood & Brass) (Your Name, "Attorney at Law")
- Compact Office Set – Portable – Small set consisting of stapler, tape, etc. (Great for the briefcase)

Bank Accounts

A law firm needs two types of bank accounts: an Operating Account and a Trust Account. Shop around for banks that are familiar with legal accounts. The Operating Account is a typical business account. The Trust account is a special account, controlled by the state and State Bar. It is referred to an IOLTA account. The state requires special and unique handling and reporting from the bank. This is why you should choose a bank that knows how to deal with this important account.

Banks are very competitive with offers to open new accounts. Look for a "No Fee Account," an account that has no monthly charges to maintain. Also, pick a bank where you are introduced to a business banker or manager. Establish and nurture a good business relationship with this person. He or she is one among many valued business professionals in your network. These people are very important to you, as a new attorney. Their advice, service, and potential referrals are very important. Get to know them on a first name basis. Send announcements, thank you letters, holiday cards, etc. to nurture the relationship.

The Operating Account is basically a business checking account. This is where you deposit all monies earned to pay for your payroll, lease, expenses, supplies, etc. You would want a check card in order to have easier and convenient access to the account. Minimize or eliminate all expenses associated with the account. Choose the free or simple low cost checks. Do not choose to pay for monthly statements, if you can access free statements online. You won't need a fancy and large check register or combination accounting system that the bank may offer you. You also do not need duplicate checks. A basic check register and basic checks work best. A basic, free, and simple account will do just fine.

The Trust Account is an important account. You must check with your State Bar regulations on how to maintain this account. The account is "strictly" for depositing your clients' money (retainer), to be drawn upon as you earn it. Do not commingle your own funds in this account. The rules are very strict and many attorneys are severely disciplined for mismanaging this account. This account requires a separate and specially structured accounting and reporting system that you are personally responsible for. Remember, it is the clients' money, not yours!

The bank must report to the State Bar about certain occurrences to this account. All interest earned in the account usually goes to the State Bar, neither you nor the client. The State Bar uses these funds for specific purposes, like free legal aid to the public, among other things. It is important that you choose a bank experienced with this type of account.

Accepting Credit and Debit Cards

Make it easy for your clients to pay you! Being able to accept credit and debit cards is one way to offer your clients a great convenience. It is a perfect way for the client to finance and be able to pay your fees. Accepting credit cards is not a big issue with most businesses, but it is a HUGE ISSUE for attorneys.

The potential conflict is accepting credit card payment for "retainer money" (money you have not yet earned). Usually, retainer funds are deposited into your Trust Account because these funds are not yet yours. It is the clients' money until you earn it.

The problem is with the merchant service provider. Most providers will want to deduct their fees from the credit card payment and deposit the rest in your account. By doing this, they are, in essence, deducting their fee from the clients' funds. This is a big No-No. So, what if you deposit your own funds in the Trust Account to cover the charges? Again, this is a big No-No, and a quick way to be severely disciplined by your state Bar for "co-mingling funds." This is not allowed in attorney trust accounts. The clients' money is to be completely separate from yours.

Be very careful to ask how the merchant charges are paid, and avoid anything other than the following:

- Set up a credit card acceptance account.
- Choose a virtual terminal option – This allows you to input the transaction on the service provider's website, and it is linked to your Operating and Trust Accounts.
- Deduction of merchant charges, for credit card payments deposited into either the Operating or Trust Account, is to be "strictly" charged to the Operating Account (Your Money). This applies to both payments made to your Operating Account (Fixed Fees immediately earned) and your Trust Account (Retainer payments for you to earn).

You will soon find that banks are not set up to accommodate attorney Trust Accounts, because of this important State Bar requirement. Check with the American Bar Association (ABA) or your State Bar for companies registered with them that can accommodate the proper credit card transaction for an attorney Trust Account. There are a few companies that specialize in serving attorneys. Check with your State Bar for any additional or special requirements that may not be detailed here.

Accounting System

You will need two accounting systems. One for your general business activities (Operating Account) and another for the state regulated accounting of your clients' funds (Trust Account).

Your general business activities can be simply recorded in a basic accounting ledger or journal. A simple system can be found in your local office supply store. Look for a common small business accounting book that when opened, shows activities by the week. The common activities to be recorded are:

- Income (Earned Fees)
- Payroll Taxes (FICA, Medicare, Federal, State & Local Taxes, Deductions, etc.)
- Payment Registry (Check and Cash)
- Business Expenses
    - Lease
    - Phone
    - Parking
    - Office Supplies

- Equipment
- License Fees
- Office Expenses (copies, fax, etc.)
- Business Subscriptions
- Etc.

Accounting for your clients' funds in your Trust Account is a different story. Each state has specific requirements as to how you should record and report activities in your Trust Account. You must check your State Bar for specific requirements.

Typically, the Trust Account system contains:

- General Ledger – All account fund activities.
- Individual Client Ledger – All fund activities pertaining to that "one" individual client. There is one separate Client Ledger per client.
- Cash Ledger – Cash Deposits (when you accept "cash" from clients)
- Deposit Ledger – All Deposits Only.
- Payment Ledger – All Payments Only.
- Reconciliation Verification Report – Signed by you, verifying the balancing of all accounts.
- Note: Other requirements may exist depending on your State Bar.

Do not stress out about the maintenance of the Trust Account. It's only your license at risk! Just kidding... But seriously, research your individual state's requirements and follow them. Your State Bar may have assistance available to help you with the correct setup. You'll be fine.

Business Attire

Image is everything! Have you heard this before? It is so true. Your client's initial perception and initial impression of you is your appearance.

Fashion has no place in the legal profession. Don't get me wrong… Quality clothing is very important. The lawyer look is very specific and should express the following and "only" the following qualities and message:

- Professional
- Conservative
- Serious
- Expensive
- Competent
- Powerful
- Confident
- Fearless
- Experienced

So, how does your appearance say all this, you ask? Very simply, the public has certain pre-conceptions of specific appearances. Everything from the way you fix your hair to your shoes, and everything in between, gives a specific perception and message. People make all kinds of assumptions at the first impression. People judge all the time based on appearance.

To decide on the message that you want to give, you need to analyze the specific conditions of the situation. Think of a potential client. They are coming to you for your professional expertise and advice. They may be worried and concerned about the legal predicament they are in. They are seeking protection, advice, confidence, and knowledge... in other words, a legal professional.

Let's begin with your personal grooming. A fresh clean look starts everything on the right track. I know this issue might sound obvious and maybe ridiculous to mention, but for the sake of those who lack the awareness, here it is. A modest and conservative look is what you are after.

For gentlemen, the hair is always short, well-styled, and clean. Faces are always clean-shaven. Facial hair is not preferred, but if you must, then it should be neat, short, clean, and meticulously trimmed. For ladies, hair is well-styled and clean. Hair length should be appropriate for the office. Make up is modest and light.

For both, gentlemen and ladies, hands should be manicured. A conservative and elegant watch is OK, but nowadays, no watch is OK, too. Jewelry is at a minimum. A ring is OK on your left hand ring finger (law school ring, wedding band, engagement ring). Absolutely no piercings! Earrings, for ladies, should be elegant and tasteful. No earrings for gentlemen. Eyeglasses should be lightweight, elegant metal frame. Lenses should be clear, no tint, and anti-glare, so the client can see your eyes.

For gentlemen and ladies, your business attire will consist of a well-tailored business suit. If you need to purchase one, invest in one that matches the following criteria. The only acceptable colors are dark charcoal grey (first choice), dark navy blue, and dark grey. Pinstripes are not necessary, but if you must, they should not be distracting and should not be visible from a short distance. Think "banker look." Absolutely no beiges, browns, or pastels. The suit should be freshly dry cleaned and pressed. The shirt or blouse is always white, freshly ironed, and starched. For men, the tie is silk. The color and design are conservative and reserved. Shoes and belts are always black leather. People notice shoes, so make sure they are polished and not scuffed. For men, they should be laced and pointed, not round at the toe. For ladies, the shoe is elegant and simple (think office, not party). Skirts are always simple, elegant and below the knee. The briefcase is always black leather, not scuffed, and elegant. It should be functional to carry files, documents, and your laptop.

Take some time and observe professional people. Be aware of the impression that the different looks give you. This will help you with your choices. The advice of a clothing consultant, like the sales representative at a business clothing store, could be helpful.

My advice here is to get you started with a proven and widely acceptable image. I'm sure that your college and law school attire was not as formal, and this will be a new experience for most of you. Start with my suggestions. As you get more exposure to the professional world, you will be more aware of the professional appearance, and will make good choices for yourself.

Chapter 3 - Finding New Clients

So, here we are. By now, you have your business structure in place. It feels exciting and a little scary, right? Stay hopeful, the next step is the most rewarding. You will now focus all your efforts on business building. We will examine various ways to attract prospective clients. At first, we will cover many cost-conscious ways to advertise, market, and promote your practice, while keeping the costs, if any, at a bare minimum. Later, as you start depositing earnings in your business account, we will cover inexpensive ways to maximize the effectiveness of your marketing. For right now, job one is to find clients to get your practice up and running.

Before we proceed, we must revisit something that will help set the tone for this chapter. From this point forward, you are an entrepreneur. Remember, the definition of an entrepreneur is someone who creates and builds a business enterprise with great initiative and risk. Entrepreneurs create something out of nothing. They are motivated to succeed. There is a fire in their belly. They hunger for results and profit. Entrepreneurs take great pride in what they create, because it is all their own. For entrepreneurs, failure is nothing to fear because they do not answer to anyone, nor do they have to explain their business decisions or results to anyone. Failure is an opportunity to learn something new. Fear is the opportunity to improve oneself and become stronger. Failure and fear are to be looked at as check points along the way of building your business. They will help you identify something you may need to improve or change. There is no need to be disappointed or discouraged. This is simply a process and an opportunity to fine-tune your strategies and plans to strengthen your efforts and help get you the desired results. No one will judge you or criticize you. The entrepreneur lives and dies by his or her own decisions.

Entrepreneurs are self-taught. This is an important quality that differentiates them from any other businessperson. They look for answers on their own, without any suggestions of when and where to start looking. They learn because they crave knowledge.

An entrepreneurial attitude sometimes manifests itself from need and frustration with the status quo. I am hoping that if you are reading this book, you already have that spark. Do the previous few paragraphs strike a special chord in you? Do you understand what I am describing? You are looking for your own place in the world. You are considering going solo for your own reasons. If these reasons motivate you to read on, you have it!

The reason I took some time to revisit the idea of entrepreneurship, is because it is a necessary quality. Many law schools have finally awakened to the reality that being a lawyer is not only a profession, but also a business. As we discussed before, some schools are teaching entrepreneurship as part of their program curriculum. I am not sure how effective the courses are in developing an entrepreneurial mind. Sure, you could learn all about entrepreneurship, but do you feel the attitude?

I think that necessity motivates. If you were running into walls, not finding employment, or not finding the type of work that interests you, you probably felt like you were getting nowhere. And now, you are thinking about employing yourself. You might think, "Why Not?" "I am smart," "I am able," I can learn how." "If other lawyers are doing it, I can too," "I just need a glimpse into the 'how to,' and I can take it from there."

Let's practice the first powerful tool of an entrepreneur. Let's visualize a scenario that would motivate you. Let's imagine what you want from a new law practice of your own. What gets your juices flowing? What are the ideal results that would give you what you think success is?

Think of yourself getting up in the morning, excited because you have a few appointments already scheduled for the day. You have a few opportunities to contract some new work. The type of work that will give you experience, confidence, and competence. The type of work that keeps you busy. Cases that you choose and not given by a boss. Cases that you price according to how you value your time. You are always well paid, because you set the fee.

Think of the pride that you have, because you are well on your way to becoming a successful young lawyer, in your own law firm. You have created a marketing plan that is working. Every time your phone rings, it is an opportunity for new business! Someone just saw your advertisement and is interested in hiring you. How would you answer the call? Within how many rings? How long would that potential client have to wait until you return their call? Would you be smiling as you answer the call? Would you be excited at the opportunity and possibilities that this call may bring?

Now we are ready to proceed.

Marketing Strategy

Marketing is the collection of plans or strategies that will help you get in front of potential clients. Think of marketing as a business toolbox. Inside this toolbox, you have various tools that will help you produce new business, from either new or existing clients. The tools look something like this:

- Market Research
- Pricing
- Advertising & Media Selection
- Presentation & Delivery
- Follow Up

As you begin to strategize, you could either research a specific area of law already in your mind, or look to identify an area that interests you. Either way, you should be open to discovering new opportunities. Remember, you are starting a new law practice. The potential for growth and stability is increased when you are servicing the legal needs demanded of your community. These are new clients that are already asking for legal help, in great numbers!

Market Research

Market research is simply finding out which legal needs are sought out by potential clients. These needs can vary and change with time and current market conditions. Many things affect market demand. Some of these are:

- Local Economic Conditions
- Local Demographics
- Divorce Rates
- Age of Population
- Real Estate Market Changes
- Employment & Unemployment
- New or Changing Laws

Local Economic Conditions

Every location or area has unique factors to its economy. Each depends on specific industries or economic draws. People living in a specific region may have similar legal needs as other people in other regions. Examples of this are:

- Divorce
- Estate Planning
- Purchase or Lease Contracts
- Etc.

On the other hand, people living in less stable economic markets may have a greater need for certain legal services than other people living in areas with a more stable economy. Examples of this are:

- Bankruptcy
- Foreclosure
- Divorce
- Etc.

You must pay close attention to the legal needs of the community that you serve. Local news media, libraries, and the internet will help you identify local trends. Your family and friends can also provide you valuable market information and personal experience. Your friends and family are members of your community and can give you personal accounts of legal needs they may have or may have had. Other people within your town or community are bound to share similarities. This will help you greatly in relating and understanding your future prospects. This research will also put your name out there to your friends and family as being a proactive attorney, concerned with their needs, as well as stating your availability. These trends are doors to business opportunities. These are snapshots of what your local market is demanding.

Every community shares the need for similar legal services. Rest assured that whatever area of the law you decide to practice in, there are clients that will need legal help. The reason for identifying local economic conditions is to highlight a specific area of law that has a greater need for lawyers who practice within it. Thus, more clients!

As an example, as I am writing this book, certain economic conditions are affecting many people. Economic uncertainty due to job stability, healthcare, housing, student loans, etc. Listen... can you hear the market crying out for specific legal help?

- Help, I'm about to lose my job. What are my rights?
- Help, I've been fired without cause. Can my employer do this?
- Help, the bank is foreclosing on my home.
- Help, I just received a letter from an attorney.
- Help, I'm being evicted from my home.
- Help, I'm trying to sell my home and need help negotiating with the buyer, bank, attorney, etc.
- Help, I'm in financial distress. Is bankruptcy an option?
- Help, I am considering divorce.
- Help, I would like to become a citizen, or have permission to work.

How can you assist the great number of people needing legal help?

New clients are not difficult to find. You must first identify who they are and what they need.

Local Demographics

Every community has a unique demographic makeup. Some areas attract a specific demographic group of people who seek the advantages of living within a specific area. These advantages could be because of many reasons:

- Climate
- Taxes
- Laws
- Politics
- Schools
- Cultural
- Entertainment
- Etc.

Negative or sudden changes to the above could bring about a different demand for legal services altogether. The key is that you should always listen to what your local market is asking for. Some needs could last a long time as well as change at any time. Just remember that change is good. It means new opportunities. Be ready to respond to these changing market demands.

There are many examples of local demographics and their specific legal needs. Maybe your local community attracts young families. A good school district and affordable housing are very important to a young family. They will come in front of complicated contracts or leases. They will encounter negotiations that may have unknown consequences. They may be interested in planning for their growing estates.

Maybe your local community attracts retired people. Careful estate planning may be very important to this group. Advice on important decisions and how the law affects them may be important. Counsel on the details of a contract dealing with insurance, social security, pensions, real estate, or an investment may be needed.

Maybe your local community attracts an affluent demographic group with specific legal needs. This group may be drawn to your area because of cultural activities, business conditions, local laws, etc. Legal assistance with investment contracts may be important. High price real estate deals may require legal help. Protection of assets through customized trusts or estate planning may be needed.

Whatever the demographic makeup, specific legal needs relative to the specific demographic group exist. Pay special attention to this area of market research because exciting and new markets are constantly being created. New markets catch business by surprise and can either severely limit the amount of clients needing your law practice or greatly improve the growth opportunities, if you are ready and willing to provide the needed legal services.

Divorce Rates

At this time, the national divorce rate is around 50%. That is one out of every two marriages end in divorce. Family law is a healthy area of practice. There are many branches to the family law tree. Some of these are:

- Legal Separation
- Prenuptial Agreements
- Domestic Partner Agreements
- Divorce
- Child Custody
- Child Support
- Alimony
- Etc.

Strongly consider working in this area of law. It is one where a great need exists. Every case is financially different. You will encounter a great segment of the population needing expedient and low cost services, as well as financially complicated cases involving large assets. Consider your customer, your abilities, and efficiency. A competent attorney who is also affordable is in great need to the client with limited financial resources. Other clients are familiar with the cost of competent legal representation and are ready and able to pay for it.

Every party in a family law case needs individual representation. A family law client may have other associated needs in the future, such as bankruptcy, foreclosure, estate planning, etc. The trust bond that is created between client and attorney is strong. If you performed good work, this client will seek your help in the future.

Age of Population

Significant aging trends create unique legal dynamics. Currently, the last wave of the baby boom generation is approaching retirement. This is a huge segment of the market. There is a greater need for elder law specialists. The following are growing areas of law dealing with an aging, large segment of our population:

- Estate planning
- Nursing home abuse
- Elder personal injury
- Insurance law
- Social Security
- Disability
- Trusts
- Real Estate purchases, sales, and leasing
- Etc.

The children of the baby boomers also have unique legal needs of their own. Recognized as the sandwich generation, this group cares for both their parents and their children. They seek legal advice on:

- Tax law
- Estate planning
- Asset protection
- Real Estate transactions
- Nursing Home abuse
- Assisted Living Contracts
- Financial Management
- Etc.

Be aware of changing laws that affect specific age groups. These changes bring about opportunities.

Real Estate Market Changes

The real estate market is like any commodities market. Demand for real estate varies depending on many factors. Our country is currently experiencing a declining housing market. Since 2008, housing values have dropped by nearly half in some markets. This means that families have lost half the value in their homes. This instability has created a domino effect in other areas of our economy. Foreclosures are on the rise at unprecedented levels. Many families are losing their homes to large banks, without knowing how to defend themselves. Currently, there exists a large number of fraud and abuse by the large banks. Many people are losing their homes, unnecessarily.

Foreclosure defense lawyers are leveling the playing field between large banks and the individual homeowner. Once unresponsive to the homeowner's request for assistance, banks now deal with lawyers hired by homeowners. These lawyers help protect the legal rights of homeowners, as well as help negotiate loan restructuring and modifications. They help keep the banks accountable, by making sure the law is followed.

New federal programs are created to assist the public with this housing crisis, and attorneys are needed to help the public navigate through negotiations with the banks. The public holds their home sacred. This is where they raised their families, invested a significant amount of their wealth, and considered it in their future planning, and where they feel secure and safe. One's home is his or her American dream. The housing crisis is destroying this once sure stability for the American family.

The federal and state governments continue to launch investigations and legal action against the large banks. Their discovery of fraud and abuse is exposing a large-scale problem. Foreclosure lawyers form a new wave of legal saviors and protectors. Their work is very important to not just their clients, but to the general public, by establishing precedent and holding banks accountable. This area of law touches a special nerve with the public. They are defending their American dream.

As you can see, just about any topic in our daily lives demands unique legal assistance. The importance of market research is obvious. In order to succeed in any business, the entrepreneur seeks to supply an answer to the market demand.

Keep listening to what the market needs, be open to adapt, and be ready to respond to the market demand, and your practice will stay busy and grow.

Pricing

The pricing of your services should reflect certain aspects of the current market conditions. Consider the following when calculating how much people will be willing to pay for your services:

- Level of demand
- Competition
- Your experience
- Economy

Be very careful of the message that you are sending with your pricing. Pricing too low may say "lack of experience." Pricing too high may encourage the client to shop. You are looking for a sweet spot in which the client perceives value. At the same time, your presentation and delivery (discussed later) should build value before you quote a price.

Level of Demand

The amount of need that exists in a certain area of the law affects the pricing to satisfy that need. Do not make the mistake of only considering the level of demand without including the other aspects listed above. For example, you may notice a great demand for bankruptcy attorneys due to an unstable economy. However, if your local market where you plan to practice is saturated with bankruptcy attorneys, your business may be limited. On the other hand, if there is a small demand for a certain area of the law, and there are not many attorneys in your area to service that demand, it may create a niche opportunity for you.

Great places where you can gauge the level of demand are:

- Local newspaper, legal notices
- Current advertisements by other lawyers
- Court case dockets
- Local news outlets
- Interviewing your local legal aid organization
- Local demographics and statistics
- Local census statistics

- Surveying friends, family and neighbors
- Etc.

Obvious demand is easy to notice. Identifying unknown demand or creating a demand takes creativity. Many people can be unaware of specific legal needs that may be immediate. They may have not considered a problem because they did not know there was one. Maybe they did not think to consult with a lawyer because they did not know of the possible downfalls of a decision that was not thought out.

The new business owner may have chosen an incorrect business structure, by operating under a fictitious name instead of a corporation or LLC. A new business that just incorporated might not consider the legal ramifications of not maintaining corporate minutes or the hidden benefit of having an attorney as its registered agent. A property manager may not be aware of how to quickly evict a bad tenant. A growing family, accumulating assets, may not be aware of how to shelter and protect them from legal liability.

These people may not know they need a lawyer until they see your advertisement describing a relevant problem. Hidden opportunities are everywhere. You just have to be observant and attentive.

Competition

Other lawyers practicing in the same local market help determine the norm of how much to charge your client. Current advertisements sometimes quote prices. It is important to understand that the typical client does not know how much certain legal services cost. Advertisements that quote prices establish a value perception in the client's mind as to what a certain legal service should be worth. If your price for that same service is comparable, there will be little resistance from the client. A higher price may require a comprehensive and educational presentation from you to help the client justify paying the higher or realistic price.

Do not be afraid to be priced higher than your competition. Your success in being able to retain a higher price depends on whether the client perceives that you are worth it. People are willing to pay more if certain conditions are met:

- They trust you
- They like you
- They feel that you understand them
- They see you as better than the other

You can find out what your competition charges very easily.

- Examine their advertisements
- Ask the potential client who is comparing
- Telephone call to survey
- Check court docket files for affidavits of attorney fees and costs.
- Check with your local or state Bar for comparable statistics.

Your Experience

Your experience may affect how much you charge for your services, but not necessarily. Remember, the client values your services based on the previously discussed set of conditions:

- They trust you
- They like you
- They feel that you understand them
- They see you as better than the other

The business savvy attorney will invest time during the initial contact with the client, making sure to establish trust and credibility. Certain mannerisms and strategic questions must be employed. A certain interaction must be enabled to appeal to the client's need to feel that they found the right attorney, for them. We will discuss this communication skill more in the Presentation and Delivery section of the book.

Even though there is a lot to say about a seasoned and experienced attorney, it is more important to the client that their selected lawyer fulfills the set of conditions listed above. Many advertisements, as a Bar requirement in most states, must state a version of the following:

Your choice of attorney should not be based solely on advertisement. Compare the lawyer's experience and credentials before making a choice to hire an attorney.

A lawyer's experience does not guarantee results, nor does it symbolize the level of the lawyer's commitment to the client's case. A new attorney must show not only competence and knowledge of the law, applicable to the client's need, but also show a commitment to fight for the client's interests and rights.

In most cases, the client does not know how to compare attorneys or where to get the necessary information. They will rely on the initial interview or consultation, so it is very important to create value in the client's mind. Otherwise, you are allowing outside factors to determine your worth.

Economy

The health of the economy determines the client's ability to pay for your legal services. If times are tough, every business experiences a drop in revenue, even more so for attorneys. Corporate and individual clients tighten their financial belt. They will be more likely to shop for that special balance between price and perceived value.

Just like any other smart business, you should consider the local economic factors. A business that wishes to continue to serve its community must adapt to be able to meet the community's needs. This will ensure your ability to service more clients. It is just plain common sense to be priced according to what the client can afford.

As I write this book, I notice certain pricing trends. A few innovative law firms are advertising "flat fee pricing" for legal services. The reasoning is that in tough economic times, the unknown is very scary to the client. A client doesn't know how many hours may be necessary to see their case through to the end.

Put yourself in the client's shoes. A divorce, once started, may cost more than one can afford. The safety of a flat fee eliminates this concern, and makes it easy for the client to choose you, instead of the other lawyer who charges by the hour. Sure, a flat fee is a risk for you. If you do not estimate a sufficient fee, you might work endlessly for little pay.

Another pricing trend is "unbundled services." This means that you break down the separate stages in a legal case and price for each individual stage. This also gives the client more perceived control of the cost, by paying as they go.

Since a new attorney may not know how to accurately estimate the duration of a specific case, it is important to research. Look up similar cases in the court dockets. You will be able to see a realistic example of the duration of the case, as well as applicable steps.

The "flat fee" or "unbundled services" models are good for the client, but may be a costly education for the new attorney until you gather some experience. By now, you know the cost of your legal education. Practical experience may cost you as well. Don't fear it. It will be valuable practical knowledge that you will be able to apply in future cases.

No matter which pricing model you use, you must never break the cardinal rule of business, especially a law practice. You must always collect your fee in advance. There is no bigger waste of valuable time than having to chase an irresponsible client for an earned fee. Trust me, don't do it! If the client cannot pay the entire fee, break up the services to match the received payment. Be careful though. In most cases, a judge may not allow you to withdraw yourself from representing a client once a court case has begun. Another idea is to allow a client to make payments towards a retainer account, in which you only start to work once a certain amount is collected.

Be open and sensitive to your local market's economy. Clients will see you as being easy to work with, proactive, and business smart.

Advertising & Media Selection

This is where we discuss actual and practical ways to get the phone ringing. Advertising can reach a broad or targeted audience. It can also be expensive or not. For the purposes of this book, we will examine low cost and effective methods to advertise for clients.

An important note before we go any further: you must review your state Bar's regulations for advertising. Adapt the upcoming methods to comply with the Bar guidelines. It is very important that you do this prior to applying any of the advertising ideas. The first mistake that many new lawyers make is to get in trouble with the Bar when it comes to advertising. Most state Bars will want you to submit samples of your advertisement to approve before you use it.

Website

Your business website is the most important advertising tool. Special consideration needs to be taken in the planning and design. This is where your new potential clients will find information about you, your firm, and your work. It serves as a great way to stay in touch with your clients as well. A well kept up website is always fresh and filled with useful information that can inform and educate.

This section will assume that you are familiar with the terminology associated with an internet website. In today's world, it would be rare not to be. If you do not feel comfortable with the technicalities of designing a website, don't worry. There are many cost-effective options.

Many of the most popular web portals have easy tools to put together a great looking website using templates. Templates allow you to simply fill in your information. The design and structure are already chosen and ready. I like this option for a few reasons. Typically, this feature is offered to entice you to use the web portal to host your site. The prices are very low for a basic site. Also, you can put together a complete site and publish it in a short amount of time.

The internet portal may even offer free site management tools to help you keep the site updated and current. The tools may also include diagnostic features that help you fine-tune the content to improve its position in the search engine results. It may also include traffic analyzing features that show you how many people looked at specific pages on your site, and for how long.

There are also web design software programs that allow you more design control when making your website from scratch. These programs vary in complexity depending on your comfort level. Many computers may already have web design software included. You may also find free downloadable trial programs to try out.

Another option is to find a website designer. These services are usually inexpensive for a basic website. You may also be able to Barter your legal services for a professionally designed website. Students are a great source for website design. A student close to graduation may need samples of professional work to present to a potential employer or client. You could be a serious reference for this student. You may be able to negotiate a very low price for a great website, and help each other out at the same time. Either way, whether you are designing the site from scratch or are having it designed, you must prepare the content.

Start by checking out the websites of other attorneys to give you an idea of what a legal website contains. As you view their websites, be aware of what catches your attention and interest. Does it convey expertise and competence? If you were a potential client, would you choose this attorney? Does the design help you navigate the entire site easily, or is it too complicated? Search a topic within the site. Does it supply good information or just headline content? Does the site appear too busy and distracting to the reader? What colors and font styles were used? Do those colors and font styles express the perceived image of a serious and professional attorney? What legal disclosures are used? What information is repeated on every page (contact info, disclosures, logo, banner, etc.)? Take notes of what works and what doesn't. This will help you or your website designer with good direction when building your website.

As you research and compare other attorney websites, keep in mind that you do not want to imitate any one site entirely. Not just because of copyright law, but because you seek originality to stand out in the client's mind. A good idea is to look at attorney websites in other states far from you for design ideas. Look for sites that communicate seriousness, professionalism, expertise, and credibility. The site should portray the attorney or firm as specialists. It must be simple to navigate and easy to find important information. Pretty soon, you will have great notes and ideas that include the best of all the sites you have seen, as well as what not to include.

The first step is to map out the different pages. Keep the potential content in mind, but it is not important in this step. Think of a basic outline. Start with the main page and then the pages that will branch out from it. Here are some examples of the pages that are individual components to your site:

- HOME PAGE: This is the first page a viewer will see. It welcomes the reader with your business greeting. It can include a company profile. It may have highlights of other pages. It may have convenient links to current and relevant legal information. It will have a directory to the other areas in the site. It must have contact information to tell the viewer how to contact you. It may have your company logo and slogan in a banner. There may be appropriate photos that show you or your services. It may ask the reader if they might have any questions about their situation, and invite them to send you a message. Usually, there is a legal disclaimer at the bottom of this and every page.

- SPECIFIC SERVICE PAGE(s): These are individual and separate pages that are dedicated to specific services or areas of the law that you work in (eg. Bankruptcy, Family Law, etc.). The page includes information of how you can help the reader in this specialty.

It may include an area or link to recent changes in the law, or relevant case law examples. The more recent and relevant information, the more the client will see that you are up to date and current on important changes that may affect their case. The design should be inviting and easy to read. Use appropriate photos to communicate your message. The page will definitely have a way for the client to contact you, as well as directory links to the other pages on your site.

- BLOG PAGE: An excellent companion to the Specific Service Pages is a Blog Page. This is a very important tool for the potential client. It not only gives them current and important legal information, but also your expert legal views and comments about the topic. It gives the client a personal interview with you, right there and then. Compare this to other attorney sites that basically include an obvious advertisement of themselves, and you can see the powerful advantage. Many new attorneys worry about not having as much experience as the competing attorney. A Blog gives you instant expertise on the subject. It gives you an opportunity to express your views, opinions, and comments about relevant topics that are important to the reader. Do not be surprised if you get business inquiries from different parts of your state, even other states. Many attorneys do maintain Blogs. It takes time to post your comments and important update information, but isn't this exactly what you would want a potential client to see? The beauty of the Blog is that it continues to be out there every day and night, working to get you new clients. Start one by either analyzing a current publicized case or a news article, or by simply providing your legal opinion about a concept in the area of law you want to work in. Make daily entries commenting on the progress or changes occurring. They do not have to be every day, but if you are not busy, take advantage of this great business building opportunity. As you get busier, make an effort to maintain current entries in your Blog. You could treat it as a daily or weekly journal that you write in at the end of the day. These daily entries attract potential clients when they search for the same information in the internet search engines. Be sure that you include relevant and specific search topics within your writing so the search engines match it to the potential clients' search request.

- WHY CHOOSE OUR FIRM PAGE: Here is where you can tell the potential client why you are the right attorney for them. Many attorneys state their years of experience, awards they won, associations they belong to, etc. Obviously, you, as a new attorney, will not have comparable accolades. However, state other strengths until you can update with experience:
  - Clerk and Intern Positions
  - Special Notice from Professors
  - Academic Awards
  - Personal Passion for this specific area of the law
  - Past and Current Research Projects
  - Current Personal Study and Research in specific legal areas

- o Current Attendance at important court cases to stay on the edge
- o Legal Courses taken on Specialized Areas of Law
- o The Law School and University you graduated from
- o Special Recognition, Honors, Degrees, and Awards achieved
- o Personal Story of how you overcame challenges, took on a specific legal area to champion, personal reason to practice law
- o Your personal interaction with every client
- o Other Languages you speak
- o Etc.

- CONTACT US PAGE: This page contains your firm's name, address, phone number, fax number, email address link, and directions to your office. Also, include an invitation for the potential client to fill out a basic form to request information or to submit a question. This is an opportunity to get back with them as soon as possible to invite them to your office for a free initial consultation.

- FAQ PAGE: The Frequently Asked Questions Page should address common and not so common questions, to make the reader aware that there may be more they may need to know. An invitation to call you or to submit an inquiry or question should be included.

The second step is to put together the content that will be on each page. Take your time here. Don't worry about not having everything you want to include. You can add to or edit the pages anytime, even after they are published. Use your notes that you compiled while comparing other websites. The important thing right now is to get your site on the internet. You will have the opportunity to edit the content at any time.

The content should be informative, current, and relevant to the potential client. Be careful not to be too pushy with too many sales pitches. One innocent invitation on the page is sufficient. Remember, the reader will be searching for information about their legal concerns. They are not looking for a salesperson. If the information is useful and informative, and you, as the author, are the perceived expert, the potential client will call you.

The third step is to come up with a design or layout. Again, your notes of the sites you looked at for ideas will help you here. Think of the page design appearance just like you would think of what suit to wear in court. It would be serious, reserved, not flashy, simple, and elegant. It would express professionalism and competence. These are the same qualities of a website design of a professional and competent attorney. If you choose to enlist the help of a designer, convey these ideas to be integrated in the design.

The final step is to publish your site on the internet, making it available for anyone to find you. By now, you should have reserved a domain name (website address, eg. www.YourFirmName.com). If you haven't chosen a domain name, you must do so now. To obtain one, first write down several choices. Then, find a domain name provider online and check for availability. If your choices are common, you may have to get creative to find an available domain name. Once found, buy it. They are very inexpensive, usually around $12 per year.

If you chose an internet portal that offered design tools, then it probably included the option to reserve a domain name. If so, you just choose publish and it's done.

If you designed the site from scratch, then look online for a website host. There are many to choose from. Research the dependability and average down times of the web host. Many internet portals offer web hosting. Compare features, dependability, and cost. The average cost is around $150 per year for basic web hosting services.

If you enlisted the help of a designer, they should be able to secure the domain name for you, as well as publish the website. You would still choose the web host and cost. An important note: Make sure that the domain name is purchased and "owned" by you. This gives you the freedom to change host or designer, and go anywhere you decide, because the domain name is yours.

Remember to check the site frequently. Keep it current and fresh with new information and updates. Solicit the opinion of your clients, family, and friends. Ask for their suggestions of how the site could be more informative and helpful. Their opinions will match future clients' opinions, so listen and act.

Search Engine Optimization

Your website is up and running. Unless someone searches for the exact information that matches the information in your website, it is only one site among millions of other sites. The more unique the information in your site (like your name or a unique area of practice) that matches the search query, the better the chance that your site will appear among the first page of search results.

But, what if you are practicing in an area where many other lawyers are practicing in, like bankruptcy, divorce, etc.? How will the client find you? What can make your website appear at the top or near the top of the search results? The answer to these questions has to do with Search Engine Optimization.

Your website must be fine-tuned to be recognized by the most common search engines. Just think of when you are searching for something online. How many pages of results do you look through, before selecting a site? Probably three pages or a few more? If your site came in after page 5, the chances that the prospective client will find you diminish by how far after the first few pages your site appears. There are many things you can do to improve search results placement.

Every search engine has its own individual criteria and method to find a website. It will determine how relevant your site's information is as a match to the search query. Based on the information it collects from your site, it will determine placement on the search results.

The next thing you need to do is to register your site with the individual search engines at their online sites. The registration is offered at different levels, from free to a cost. For now, register for free. Later, you may want to try out the advertising response rate of the more popular search engines and see if it works for you.

Social Networking

Social networking sites offer great opportunities. Design and create a social networking profile. Structure it to inform and attract potential clients. Make sure that you list every possible group or network that you are or were a member of. The categories are:

- Law School
- College or University
- Fraternity or Sorority

- Sports that you played
- School Teams
- Clubs
- Professional Associations
- Etc.

This will make easy for others to find you. If you are already a member of a social networking site, now is the time to reconnect with "everyone." Let them know about your new practice, and that you are available to them when they need you. Invite them to follow you on the site, as well as check in for helpful legal updates. Your site should also link to your website and your blog, and have your office address and phone number.

The other benefit of having a presence in a social networking site is that you can search for anyone by specific categories. Just about everyone is an active member of a social networking site. Here are some ideas for useful searches:

- Age Groups (wills, estate planning, insurance contracts, etc.)
- Students (student loan contracts, job offer agreements, apartment leases, etc.)

- New Businesses (legal structure and requirements, registered agent, legal compliance)
- Category Keywords (foreclosure, bankruptcy, divorce, injured, car accident, lawsuit, etc.)
- Locality (geographical area where you practice)
- Etc.

You could search for any category or keyword. Matches of people, whose listings contain the search keyword, are listed, ready for a "hello" message from you.

Business Cards

Business cards are a basic and very effective marketing tool. The look should be simple, elegant, and professional. The card stock should be matte white or light elegant linen. It should contain ink of only one color, and no gimmicky graphics. A logo is OK, but only if it is simple and professional. Shop around for a small print shop that would be delighted to have you as a new client. The personnel should be knowledgeable and their recommendations tasteful and appropriate. Remember, any print piece is a reflection of you. It should state professional, competent, and serious. Include a business card in any mailing to potential clients. Pass them out when appropriate, to network with other professionals that may refer you a new client.

Announcements

The first group of people to reach out to is family and friends. Again, check with your local state Bar for advertising rules on contacting people who already know you. This announcement should be formal, similar to announcing a special event. If within budget, have it professionally prepared. If not, then office supply stores carry blank announcements that you can produce in your laser printer. Stick to a who, what, when, and where format. Let the print shop personnel guide you to find the appropriate look and style, for a serious law firm. Include a few business cards with the announcement. This will let everyone who knows you know that you are open for business.

Newsletters

Newsletters are a great way to stay in touch with past clients, potential clients, family, and friends. After you send out the first announcement, there may be a long time before the recipient might need you. If you disappeared from memory, they may contact someone else. Newsletters keep your name out there, always provide important information, support your credibility as an expert, and always let the reader know that you are only a phone call or email away. Unlike a website that needs to be found, a newsletter is mailed and emailed directly to the person. I say mailed and emailed because it doubles the effectiveness that it will be seen. Also, since you produced it on your computer, it is a minimal effort to save it as a PDF, and email to your groups of contacts (family, friends, clients, prospects, referral sources).

Newsletters could be as simple as an 11" x 17" paper, folded to a standard 8.5" x 11" size. Most office utility software includes a publishing program that can help you design the newsletter. It could be sent out monthly or quarterly. Understand that if you commit to a frequency of mailing, your readers will expect it. If you change from monthly to quarterly, announce the change in the newsletter a few months before you do. It should be a light read, informative, and relevant. Pick out topics that are current and relevant to many. Stay away from topics that may alienate people, such as religion or politics. Simply state a legal issue that is current in the news and simplify how it may be a problem or solution to your reader. Your legal opinion is valuable, as well as a strong introduction and presentation to the reader.

The news is a good way to pick topics. The newsletter's efficiency will improve if it covers an issue already in your readers' minds. Do not promote yourself or advertise your services. Only inform and assist. This will send a message that you are a professional attorney, who is knowledgeable and passionate about the topics covered. It is enough to include all your contact information at the end of the newsletter. You could include a link to your blog or website for more information or future update on the topic. Just remember to provide more information and updates soon.

Flyers

A flyer can be as simple as a text-only announcement on a blank sheet of paper to a full-color production. A simple word processor or publishing program can be used to create it.

Use the flyer to communicate anything. Here are some examples:

- Legal Specialty
- Promotion
- Legal Seminar
- Free Consultation
- Your New Location
- Etc.

The flyer should contain all your contact information, including address, phone number, email address, website, fax, blog, etc. As a matter of fact, every piece of advertising should include all your contact information. This invites the potential client to reinforce his or her curiosity and need to know you better before the request for your services. The multiple inquiries add credibility to your professionalism and expertise.

Flyers can be included in other mailings. They can be posted on bulletin boards or left on information tables. They can be mailed by themselves. They are inexpensive to produce; from your computer printer, as you need them, to having hundreds or thousands made at a local print shop for pennies per copy.

Letters

Yes, a simple letter can also be a great opportunity to offer your services. With the help of mail merging capability of your word processing software, you can mass-produce elegant and customized letters directed to an individual. Again, be sure to check with your local legal Bar for requirements for legal advertising. For example, in my area, the letter and envelope are required to have a red typed message that states "legal advertising." Another Bar requirement may be for the advertising letter to state your qualifications, experience, or education.

The advertising letter starts with your introduction. It follows with a description of a legal solution to a problem. Then, it ends with your offer to assist with the problem. It is simple and to the point.

Letters can be sent to past clients, family, and friends. You can also compile an address list of prospects. The contacts may be gathered from many sources:

- Prospect Calls to your office
- Past Clients
- Family & Friends
- Blog Subscribers

- Social Network Friends
- Property Appraiser website
- Mailing Lists from list brokers
- Canvassing neighborhoods
- Phone Directories
- Etc.

These address lists can be used many times over. If there are any changes, the returned envelopes will identify which ones need to be deleted or changed in your list. Maintain your address list in a spreadsheet program that can be merged with your word processor. These lists can be used for different media, like flyers, newsletters, announcements, etc.

Brochures

Brochures should be professionally produced. You can design and create with a publishing program, but have it produced at a local print shop. The reason is that you want a professional finished product. One can tell if it was printed with a laser or ink jet printer. It will not be the image you want to project to prospective clients.

A brochure must be a light read. It must contain images or graphics, as well as a summary message. Within it, invite the reader to visit your website for more information. You should collect and critique brochures that you receive in the mail or pick up. Write notes in the brochure of what works and what does not. Pay attention to the design. Does it maintain your attention or lose you? Ask the assistance of your friends and relatives for their opinions of what makes the brochure effective and influential, or not.

Your brochure, like your website, should express professionalism, credibility, and seriousness. It would not be a bad idea to use information and images from your website. It is smart to tie in your various advertising media to express the same message. Let each piece support the other. The similarity helps the prospective client retain your message and thus makes your efforts more effective.

Internet Directories

Internet directories have almost replaced the traditional phone book. Even though the phone book is still distributed, its cost to advertise may be prohibitive to a start-up business with a limited advertising budget. Later on, you may consider the phone book to reach a segment of the population, such as older generations who are not comfortable with the internet.

There are many internet directories, so how do you choose which one? The answer is all of the relevant ones. A good marketing research strategy might be to just do an internet search for any area of the law, like "criminal lawyer" for example. Note, that within the individual websites of specific attorneys, you also see listings in directories. The lawyer advertising in the directory just improved his or her chance of being found. Maybe their website or contact information did not make the first few pages in the search results, but it did appear in the directory site. Do you see the effectiveness? Make various test searches. Search the area of the law that you are practicing in. Write down all of the individual directory names. Later, go to the directory sites and sign up for the free listing.

Internet directories optimize their site to appear among the top of the search results list. They design their list to make it attractive to the person searching, who will then click on their site. One aspect that helps optimize their ranking is consumer comments. The more comments that a listed business has, the more attractive it is to the person searching. The comments, especially the positive ones, reinforce the prospective client's selection. This will better the chance that they will call you. Whenever you receive a call from a prospective client, you should always ask how they heard of your firm. This information is like gold to you. It will help identify what advertising is working. You should also make a note in the client's file, so you can ask them for a comment of their experience in the directory. A happy client will be more than willing to share their positive experience, but be careful; an unhappy client will be glad to comment as well.

Directory listings need to be checked occasionally to make sure that the listing information is current and accurate. Always make sure to include images or additional information, if allowed. Take advantage to maximize the effect of your directory listing. Offer a free initial consultation; include a link to your website, etc. Create a listing in every relevant directory. This is effective free advertising.

Press Release

News reporters seek expert opinions to help explain their story to their readers. Be on the lookout for news topics that have relevance with laws that affect them. Select a few reporters that have a regular column or space on a news source. Examples of local news sources are:

- Newspaper
- Magazine
- Newsletter
- Cable News Chanel
- Network TV Chanel
- News or Talk Radio
- Internet News
- Etc.

Prepare a legal view or opinion, written in language that is easy for anyone to understand. Avoid complex legal language. Help the news reporters by clarifying and explaining how the news topic affects their readers. Your expert and professional opinion and view is valuable to the news reporter, who also tries to be of value to his or her readers and, just as important, the boss or editor.

Submit these press releases regularly, and often, even if your opinion is not used. The important goal is to make yourself known to the reporter as an available source, in case they need you. When the reporter contacts you, it could be huge. Imagine reaching the thousands of readers or TV audience, as a local legal expert, instantly credible, and just a phone call away.

Press releases from experts sometimes turn into interviews and guest spots on TV and radio shows. The results to your law practice are priceless. Search the internet for radio shows that feature an "ask the attorney" portion of the show. Listen to it to learn the format and topics covered. Some radio markets already include these types of shows. Your area may not, and you may be the first. If not, remember that there are many channels on the dial.

You benefit from all of this exposure to potential clients, for free. If your opinion gets published, or your TV or radio interview is aired, you can also list them as accomplishments or expert work in the qualifications area of any other advertisement. Being a legal contributor or consultant is very prestigious. To the potential client, it means that a news source with thousands of readers or viewers, maybe even the prospect, chose your valuable opinion as an important part of their story. This will enhance your credibility and advantage over other lawyers. Best of all, other news sources may contact you as well. Take advantage of this opportunity. It is free, and the effectiveness is big!

Online Videos

Posting a video online is free. There are many video sites that contain anything from music videos, comedy, shows, etc. Videos that match search inquiries also appear on the search results list. They can be instructional, informative, self-help, etc. Here are some ideas:

- Video Seminars on various topics
- Free Video Initial Consultations
- Teachings on various legal topics
- Explanation of legal terms
- How to Videos (Small Claim, Quit Claim Deed, etc.)
- Video Tours of the Local Courthouse
- Etc.

The video should contain contact information or links that the viewer could click on. Name the video something general, then the specific title like "New York Bankruptcy" – "What is Chapter 7?" This will increase the possibility of matching search inquiries.

Online videos are a great way for potential clients to meet you. You have a chance to rehearse and preview how you look. Fine-tune the video so that the client sees you at your best. Record many takes, experimenting with the suit fabric, your tie, the location, the lighting, the sound, etc. Maybe you can find a media student who can use your videos in their resume or portfolio.

Set up a video library online. You could even ask your clients to view them, as an extra service. The videos should be informative enough so that the potential client has to call you for more specifics, applicable to their unique situation.

Books and Pamphlets

Materials that you self-publish accomplish many things. The publications may actually sell and create additional income. The publications are also credits to your qualifications and expertise. A well-researched book or pamphlet creates credibility. It gives you the image of an expert in your field, and on the cutting edge of the area of law. Previously, we discussed TV and radio shows. Send them a copy of the book!

The topics for your book can be instructional, self-help, and informative. Here are some examples:

- How to file a small claim lawsuit in your state

- Purchasing Real Estate
- How to Write a Will
- Leasing an Apartment in your state
- Etc.

Writing a book can be a natural and easy way to learn about a topic that you are researching. The book is simply a collection of your notes. Self-publishing through an online book seller is free. You upload the file and design the cover, and the book seller prints it on demand, when orders come through. The book seller even provides the market and site for buyers to purchase. It is a great way to build your credibility, add exposure, and again, it is free!

Politicians

Campaigning politicians offer an excellent opportunity for business. Tight campaign operational budgets make the new attorney, with little overhead and lower fees, a practical investment for the campaign manager. There are many tasks that a new attorney can provide, at a lower cost than hiring an established firm. Some examples are:

- Legal Research

- Compliance with applicable laws
- Election Rules
- Preliminary Legal Work
- Outside Counsel
- Fund Raising Laws & Guidelines
- Filing Appropriate Forms
- Legal Liaison
- Press Management
- Speech Writer
- Disclosure
- Policy Position of Candidate
- Etc.

As you can see, a new lawyer can be very valuable and useful to a campaign. The work can lead to plenty of opportunities down the road. The experience gained is valuable to other campaigns in the future, or other locations. The business contacts that will be made are priceless. The trusting and effective service that you provided may be requested of you later, when the candidate is a working politician.

To seek out this work, simply show up to the campaign headquarters. Start by offering a mix of free and paid work. This puts you in the door. You can create value for yourself by the quality and timeliness of your work, and attitude. Even if you are not interested in a political future, remember that this is an investment on your part. Diversity and the chance to learn something new keeps work interesting, and the opportunities door open.

Outsourcing

Other lawyers are a great way to obtain extra work. Target any firm, large or small, for outsourcing work. The nature of business flow is that it is unpredictable and irregular. A firm may be currently prepared with proper staffing, but a temporary surge of business can create pressure. It may not be practical to hire and train new staff. It makes financial sense to outsource. A new lawyer is very attractive to a temporarily busy firm. Freshly-trained and eager for new business, the new attorney aims to please. Here are some examples of work you can do:

- Legal Research
- Partial Case Work
- Depositions
- Court Appearances
- Cover Time Off – Vacations & Emergency

- Review and Examine Discovery Items
- Write Legal Memorandums
- Draft Pleadings and Motions
- Etc.

You will find that as you start getting busier, you will also turn down work. Either because you simply do not have the time, or it is legal work that you don't enjoy. This is why outsourcing is so common. Look for and contact local attorneys, and maintain a list. Send something on a regular basis, like a flyer, letter, business card, announcement, etc. They may not need you now, but having your name and offered availability when they need help will assure a better chance that it will be you they call.

Referrals

Would you refer a client to just anyone? Of course not. A business relationship would need to be created and nurtured. A familiarity and trust of your work and ability needs to exist. People refer clients, friends, and relatives to people they know and trust. There are four referral sources that you need to develop business relationships with:

- Other Business Professionals
- Clients
- Friends
- Family

Other business professionals include other lawyers, accountants, medical doctors, insurance agents, real estate agents, bankers, or anyone whom you have done business with. It is very proper to ask other people who you have offered your business, to refer anyone they know who needs a lawyer. Simply hand them a business card, and mention "I appreciate the great work (or service) that you have done for me; here is my card, in case you or someone you know needs a good lawyer." Carry your business card at all times and use them when appropriate.

A happy client will always be willing to tell anyone they know about your great service. However, you must be fresh in their mind. You can stay in their thoughts by regular scheduled contact. A perfect way to stay in touch is a planned marketing campaign:

- Newsletter
- Holiday Cards
- Birthday Greetings
- Congratulations Greeting
- Thank You Cards

- Occasional Hello and How Are You Letter
- Thank You Gift
- Follow Up Material

There are many reasons to stay in touch, especially with past clients. Many lawyers perform a service and then forget the client. This type of business is always on the hunt for new business. The smart lawyer knows that he is also a business. The smart lawyer stays in touch with past clients, and nurtures deeper relationships, because he knows that friends rely on and recommend each other. Trust me on this, your life will be fuller and well-rewarded proportionately to the number of people who hold you in good regard.

Court Dockets

Your local courthouse is your best source for case research and finding new business. As a new lawyer, you lack practical experience. Researching cases in your local courthouse will reveal not only procedure and sample pleadings and motions, but case strategy. A case view will allow you to examine the progression or conclusion of a case, similar to one you may be working on, or are learning. Did you also know that the courthouse records could be a great source of new business?

Most litigants that you see in most cases are potential clients for you. The court dockets are full of pro-se, or unrepresented Plaintiffs, Defendants, and Accused. Some are surprised by the service of summons and are thinking about hiring legal help. Others start litigation pro-se, and later are overwhelmed and unprepared to continue representing themselves. All these people are potential clients!

To find contact information for the parties that you want to offer your services to, simply look at the summons. The summons contains the name and address of both parties in a lawsuit. You may reach out to them through an advertising letter or flyer. Be sure that your mail piece and message complies with your local law Bar's guidelines for new prospect contact requirements. Most courthouse records are computerized and easily accessible at the courthouse's electronic records room, via their computer terminal.

Newspaper

The newspaper contains multiple sources for new business. You just have to be creative. Here are some examples:

- Legal Notices (lawsuits, land acquisions, proposed development)

- Real Estate Sales (new or modification to will, life insurance contracts, trusts, estate planning, etc.)

- New Births (insurance contracts, estate planning, college fund contract, real estate contracts or lease, etc.)

- Obituaries (probate a will, insurance contract, real estate sale, medical malpractice, etc.)

- Work Promotions (real estate contracts, employment agreement, insurance contract, etc.)

- Constructive Service (unknown or missing defendants, search for potential heirs, etc.)

- Etc.

The internet is replacing the newspaper. However, many legal notices and various listings are required to be in newspapers. It remains an excellent source for new business for the innovative and creative business person.

Contact information is sometimes stated in the listing. If not, a name is usually given. You can search online or on the local property appraiser's website for a search of address. A simple flyer or letter is appropriate for contact. Again, check with your local law Bar for contact regulations.

Sheriff's Website

A sheriff's website is frequently updated with current cases involving individuals who may need legal representation. No one thinks of having a lawyer in anticipation of an unplanned arrest or brush with the law. However, when a person is faced with an arrest, an attorney is needed. You must act fast with these sheriff listings. Search for the client, before they search elsewhere for a lawyer. Here are some examples of sheriff reports:

- DUI arrests (legal representation)
- Burglaries (criminal defense)

- Domestic Calls and Arrests (injunctions, divorce, custody, lawsuits, etc.)
- Narcotics Searches (legal representation)
- Etc.

Seminars

Seminars are an effective way to find new clients. They could be conducted at any business facility or a conference room you can rent. Conference room time may even be included at your virtual office facility. Instructional and informative seminars are welcomed at businesses wishing to inform their staff or even their clients. Some seminars you may charge for, but others offered for free are a good investment of your time. Here are some examples:

- Senior Centers (estate planning, social security or Medicare issues, domestic abuse, caregiver abuse, elder law, etc.)
- Assisted Living Facilities (same as above)
- Senior Daycare Facilities (same as above)
- High Schools (career information for student and parent, debate team, law changes, etc.)

- Corporate Business (employee education, compliance information, sexual harassment in the workplace, etc.)
- Colleges and Universities (educational, policy, legal topics, law changes, financial aid, etc.)
- Etc.

Preparing and producing a seminar is very simple. Design an outline of the topic and content you want to cover. Consider any time limits in putting together a presentation. Prepare hand-outs or a course manual with your contact information. Prepare visual aids. Have plenty of business cards handy. Allow time for questions, answers, and discussions. If you are providing the room, make sure that enough seating is available, as well as refreshments. Announce the seminar a few times before the date.

Offer your time right after the seminar for potential consultations. Be sure that you can provide privacy, or just invite them to schedule a consultation at your office, their home, or by telephone at a later date. Make sure everyone registers, either prior to or at the seminar. Follow up with all attendees with additional information and an invitation to a free initial consultation.

Chapter 4 - Keeping Clients and Building Your Practice

This chapter is the key to having a thriving and growing business. The difference between businesses that continually struggle to obtain new clients, and those that do not need to advertise as much, is how clients are valued and treated. If you remember from Chapter 3, we discussed the components of a marketing strategy. In this chapter, we will continue with the last two components:

- Presentation & Delivery
- Follow Up

Many businesses stop at the last chapter, maybe because of laziness, or because they get too busy quickly and neglect to keep prospecting. The rush in business soon slows down, and then one must hunt again. This creates a roller coaster effect in the flow of clients. It makes for a very inefficient use of time and it will keep you always rebuilding. The better strategy is to continuously market to stay in touch with past clients and advertise for new ones.

Past clients are the life blood of a sustainable business. These are people who are already sold on your service. If you did your job right, as we will discuss later, they will continue to trust you. They will brag about what a great lawyer they have, to anyone and everyone. New business, in the form of referrals, is the solid kind and best of all, it's free! If you continue to nurture and care for your past clients, your business will grow exponentially. But the key is that you have to do it continuously, without fail. It is very easy for the client to forget you in time, if you are out of sight and mind.

Presentation & Delivery of Service

The method of presentation and delivery of service should be given some serious thought. Think of the difference of how you are treated in a basic business transaction. Let's say, you pull up to a drive-through window at a fast food restaurant:

Example 1:

- *Can I take your order?*
- *That'll be $$$, pull up.*
- *Here you go. (Rushed off).*

Example 2:

- *Good Morning! Thank you, for your visit today! Have you decided on your order?*
- *Let me repeat your order, to make sure I have it right... Is that correct?*
- *Would you like to try ...? They're fresh out of the oven!*
- *OK, your total is $$$. Please pull up to the window.*
- *Here is your order. Thank you, so much. Do you need extra napkins or condiments? OK, have a great day... Please come back soon!*

See the difference? It is the same product, same price, same transaction, and same expectation at first, but different impression at the end. This is what I mean by thinking of how you present and deliver your service. You can choose to just produce what you are hired to do, or make a small effort to leave a lasting impression. There is a business wisdom that goes like this: always under promise and over deliver.

There are basic elements to the client's perception and impression of you. The choice of what and how you express these elements depends on the client's expectations. Just think of what the client may be expecting, both obvious and not so obvious. People, for the majority, do not meet lawyers on a regular basis. Their perceptions may be based on what they see on television, what they have heard from other people, their past experience, or what they hope to find. It may be a mixture of all or some of these. Either way, something or someone has formed his or her expectations and opinions about meeting you, before he or she have even set eyes on you:

- Serious Professional
- Suit, Tie and, Briefcase
- Well-spoken
- Well-versed in the Law
- Busy
- Successful Appearance
- Has the Right Answer

The client's not so obvious expectations and hopes:

- Protector
- Defender & Guardian
- Confident, Knowing, & Strong
- Understanding & Caring
- On My Side

The initial client meeting is your opportunity to learn the client's expectations, and then you must plan to exceed them. But how do you know their starting point? A pre-meeting questionnaire may be a good tool. Think of when you first meet a new doctor. You probably filled out a pre-consultation questionnaire, detailing your medical history, ability to pay, what medical problem brought you there, and if you were referred, and by whom. It seems natural to give this information to your doctor because you will be relying on their care. The same holds true for you, the attorney.

There is an old adage that holds a lot of truth, "confide honestly with your priest, your doctor, and your attorney!" The client already wants to confess it all. You just have to ask. Create an initial consultation questionnaire for the client to fill out prior to your meeting. This will state the client's problem and expectations. Include questions that will help you present and deliver what the client is expecting.

See, it's not hard. You don't have to be a mind reader. Here are some sample questions:

- *Are you currently represented by an attorney?*
- *Have you ever been represented by an attorney? If yes, for what?*
- *Name, address, phone numbers, email addresses.*
- *Please explain what type of advice or information we may help you with today?*
- *What other parties may be involved?* (this question will help you determine if there is a conflict of interest)
- *Describe the situation or concern that brought you here today?*
- *Have you discussed this matter with an attorney, prior to this visit? If yes, did you hire that attorney? If no, why not?*
- *In the best case scenario, what do you hope will happen with this situation?*
- *How will you be paying for this consultation today? Check, Credit Card, Cash?*
- *How did you learn of our office?*
- *Etc.*

Now, let's see how you can fine-tune your presentation and delivery of service, relating to your personal appearance, your office, and your work.

Personal

The main product you are selling is you. It is not enough to just be professional, as most lawyers are. To leave a lasting impression, you must pay attention to the details that form the client's image and perception of you. Without the client's positive experience of these details, you will be lost in the crowd. To be remembered, you must stand out.

We covered self-image and attire at the end of chapter 2. In this chapter, we will discuss other facets of you and your business that state a message to your client. These are:

- First Impressions
- Mannerism
- Work Ethic
- Credentials
- Memberships
- Experience
- Community Involvement

First Impressions

The first contact with a potential client is what motivated them to initiate a call to you. This may have been your website, an advertisement, or a referral. Be sure to pay special attention to the suggestions discussed in the previous chapter, to ensure that the correct initial message is delivered.

The next contact with a potential client is the phone call. A busy and successful law office may pick up the call on the third or fourth ring. The person answering the phone should be someone other than you, maybe an assistant or receptionist. Again, check with the leasing manager of your virtual office to see if they provide call answering service.

This sets the tone of a well-staffed and well-prepared law office. The voice should be pleasant, friendly, and professional. You should test the way your phone is answered by calling your office yourself. Call other law offices and compare the delivery, then adjust your receptionist's approach.

You want to have a standard greeting. Something like, *"Good morning, thank you for calling the Law Office of ____. This is ____, how may I help you?"* Always have the receptionist refer to you as Attorney _____. If you are not available, the caller should be told that you are currently with a client, in court, or just stepped into a meeting. The caller should be assured that his or her message will be delivered to you as soon as you become available.

The receptionist should have a standard message form to collect the necessary information for you to be effective when you return the call. The questions should be simple and brief:

1. What is your name?
2. What number can Attorney _____ reach you at?
3. What type of legal case does this involve?
4. What questions would you like for me to relay to Attorney _____?
5. How did you learn of our office?

Assuming that you are a one person operation, do not have the receptionist schedule appointments. When you return the call, you will have the opportunity to qualify and determine if it merits an office visit. Initial calls are not for consultations. They are to gather information and to determine if you can be of service, and whether a client wants to hire you. They are a lead in to schedule an office consultation, either paid or free. This could be determined at the initial call.

Examples of free consultations are:

- Basic Information & Qualification

- Determine the scope of work
- Determine if you could help
- Determine fee amount
- Never give legal advice
- Schedule an office appointment to execute a fee agreement or a paid consultation.
- Anything else is a paid consultation! Remember, payment is due at arrival, before the consultation.

Mannerisms

The client expects his or her attorney to be an effective communicator and to possess superior business etiquette. This expectation also serves as a qualifier to the potential client. Your communication skills and professional manners that your client experiences directly express how you will represent the case to other related parties, opposing counsel, the jury, and the judge. It will also give the client a glimpse at your approach to how effective you may be with influence and negotiations.

Effective communication is more than just conversation. It includes a proper mix of verbal and non-verbal communication. It involves effective listening and confirmation that both sides understand the message being communicated. It involves good manners and professional etiquette to accent the message. Superior professional manners begin with the basics:

- Always be "on time" for any appointment or meeting. Also, be mindful of how long the meeting is expected to last. Everyone's time is very important.

- If possible, have the client brought to you by the receptionist or assistant. If not, it is OK to come to the lobby and receive them. If this is a scheduled paid consultation, payment should be collected now.

- Initiate eye contact with a welcoming smile to engage the other person.

- Always stand to greet a person, maintaining eye contact and a welcoming smile.

- Stand up straight, and don't rush your movements. Be confident and assured.

- Be the first to extend an offer of a hand shake.

- The handshake should be firm, but don't squeeze. Maintain eye contact.
- Greet client by Mr. and/or Ms. (all women are greeted as Ms., unless you know, for a fact, that she is a Mrs.)
- Show the client where to sit. If the client is elderly, it is polite to assist them by pulling out the chair for them, taking their coat, or walking cane.
- Before you take your seat, offer the client a beverage, and have the assistant get it.

A proper greeting and welcome sets the initial tone for the remainder of the meeting. You have shown professionalism, friendliness, and personal consideration for the client's needs. It is a good start.

Next, you need to take control of the meeting by offering structure, concern, and interest. At this initial consultation, you will need to learn the client's main points of concern. A determination, whether the client has a legal case or not and if you can help them resolve their problem, must be made. You must estimate a plan of action and a reasonable fee for your services. At the same time, how you accomplish the above is just as important. Here are a few suggestions of the proper mannerisms for good listening:

- Review any previous relevant communication, before commencing with the meeting's agenda.
- State the time you have set aside for this meeting (should be a reminder of what you told them when setting this meeting).
- Allow necessary time for the client to fully explain their concerns.
- Confirm what is said by repeating the main points back to the client.
- At the end, say, "Before ending our meeting, do you have any other issues you would like to discuss?" (could be more business)
- Take notes throughout the meeting.

Work Ethic

Value what you do! It will be obvious to everyone around you. This means your clients, your potential clients, your employees, your friends, and family. Your enthusiasm and passion is contagious, and therefore a very powerful tool to set a professional tone for those in your circle of influence. It will make you memorable and keep you in demand.

Value time! Respect your time, and that of your clients. Time truly is money. Nobody appreciates their time being wasted. Be on time for your appointments and meetings. People will notice your commitment and seriousness.

Return calls promptly. When the phone rings, it is because people need to speak with you at that moment. If you can't speak to them then, return their call as soon as possible and thank them for waiting. Potential clients expect you to be busy, but accessible. When you don't return calls within a reasonable time, you are giving the message that you are "too busy," and not available. It is the surest way to lose clients. Have a personal policy to always return the day's calls before ending your day.

Your word is your bond. Delivering less than what you promise, or what the client expects, are a disappointment and a failed delivery. Set realistic expectations and strive to surpass them. It will leave a memorable impression. It is always better to under promise and over deliver. Remember this.

Emphasize quality with everything you do. The difference between average and superior is sometimes just a small additional effort. Why not deliver quality, all the time? The extra effort will be noticed and remembered. Demand that anyone or anything, associated with you and your image, always perform at their best, or not at all.

Organization is the key to efficiency. Manage your time with a good day organizer. Use it always. Do not start your day until you have reviewed it to see what is planned. Do not end your day until you plan out any upcoming events or tasks. You will find that you will have more time available and less time wasted. More time means more quality of life, and more time for new business. Time is the true luxury in life.

Credentials, Memberships, & Experience

Potential clients use your credentials and any associations as a qualifying tool when choosing a lawyer. Who and what you associate yourself with speak volumes. It states a commitment and passion about the mission of the group or committee. Join associations that mirror an interest or area of law you practice in. Also, join associations to learn about areas of law you may be interested in.

Any membership is a credential. Because you may be new to practicing law, any credential is beneficial. Just as experience will help you sharpen your skills, networking with other professionals and learning from them will help you as well. Many associations are learning opportunities. Since you have to maintain a continuing education requirement, these membership seminars or classes may offer education credits towards it.

Existing clients will need to know about any new areas of practice that you can help with. The past client will value and remember your commitment to specialize in any area of law that they may need help with later. New memberships or new classes are an excellent reason to stay in touch with past clients.

Community Involvement

There are many ways you could help your community. There are many people who can't afford to hire an attorney when they truly need one. Your state Bar may require you to provide a certain amount of pro-bono hours to your community. Many lawyers see pro-bono as just a requirement. Savvy attorneys and firms see it as an opportunity.

Pro-bono work makes a noble credential. It also opens new doors with potential clients that you may be able to help on a contingency basis, maybe right away or later. Work on contingency can be very lucrative. Here are some examples:

- Personal Injury
- Slip and Fall
- Social Security Disability
- Foreclosure
- Collections
- Etc.

Just about any work, in which the court may award attorney's fees, can be offered on contingency. This way the client who can't pay presents you with an opportunity to earn a fee, paid by the opposing party, if you prevail in the case.

Charities and non-profits will always welcome free legal help. They may even list your name as a sponsoring attorney, giving you exposure to the many beneficiaries of the organization. It is like a strong referral. The people that the charities help will see you as a professional with the same interest and concern. Do you see the advantage or edge this gives you over other attorneys, when these people need legal help with any matter? You can also include the many people and organizations that support the charity or non-profits. Some community need areas are:

- Legal Aid
- Homelessness & Housing
- Abuse (Elderly, spousal, child, animal, etc.)
- Food Banks
- Animal Shelters & Adoption
- Poverty
- Illnesses
- Free Medical Clinics
- Rehabilitation (Youth, adults, etc.)
- Etc.

Free legal seminars are a great service to a community. Specific issues affecting your community may create a need for community education. These seminars also show you in a caring and professional light to the seminar attendees, the people who may read your advertisements or flyers. If you offer a free legal seminar to a group or organization, they will promote it to their members. Again, this gives you valuable exposure to potential clients, as well as creates a credential for you. Here are some examples of organizations that may welcome your free seminars, or be interested in paying you for them:

- Senior Centers
- Retirement Communities
- Assisted Living Facilities
- Community Centers (CYO, YMCA, Etc.)
- Women and Family Shelters
- Churches
- Clubs
- Schools (PTA, clubs, etc.)
- Neighborhood Homeowner Associations
- Professional Associations
- Individual Businesses
- Etc.

Office

Your office is an extension of your image. To the client, an attractive office expresses prestige, success, experience, and competence. The appearance and staffing of your office needs special attention as a well-planned advertising piece. It will create a baseline for comparison with other attorneys before the client even meets with you.

Earlier in the book, we discussed the advantages of a virtual office setup to a limited budget. Usually this type of operation offers all the essentials of a successful office. Choose one carefully with the eyes of a potential client, as well as a returning client. Make sure that access is convenient, with a good location, comfortable lobby, professional and friendly receptionist, good parking, and frontage.

An office with poor image will work against your efforts to portray a good impression. It states carelessness, no interest, and little attention to detail, low price, less competent, second-rate, and novice. It may be a good idea to bring different people with you when shopping for office space or fine-tuning your existing one.

Work

The work you produce is the end result of why you were selected and hired. The quality and the amount of time and research that is put into your work may go unnoticed by the client. Like the way a fine wine, a painting, or architecture may appeal to the trained senses of a person who appreciates it, a client's perception of you may be disappointing if you do not educate them on the quality and amount of work you have provided.

A client should be involved and educated in the production of your work. By carefully educating the client regarding their legal situation and the legal consequences of the wrong or insufficient approach to its solution, you help develop their sophistication and their ability to appreciate your work. In essence, you can help create value for your services. You are teaching them how to appreciate your abilities and skills. Other attorneys may be equally skilled or even more so than you. If their client does not perceive it, it is not so in the client's opinion and experience. The attorney's advantages go un-noticed and wasted.

Ongoing communication with your client, about their situation's challenges and progress, will be very welcomed. It will help relieve their anxiety and strengthen their trust and confidence in you, and isn't that what they are paying for? It is amazing to me how good clients are lost due to the average value of service they experienced, when the opposite is true. But, it is the professional's fault for not educating the client on how serious or dangerous their initial situation really was, and how the professional skillfully saved them from a bad fate. Do not waste the effectiveness of the great work you do. Communicate and educate!

Follow Up

The secret of a business that keeps its past clients and grows by referrals and new business is its discipline to maintain contact with past clients and maintain the marketing plan to attract new clients. It is as simple as that. The word discipline is used because it is very easy not to do the above as you get busy. However, if you are serious about stabilizing and growing your business, you must stay in touch with past clients and continue to attract new ones.

What if you can't handle any more business? Wouldn't you love to have this problem? Well, if your business intention is to grow your practice, it will be time to hire some help. You could hire an assistant or paralegal. You should also examine the use of your time, and organize it so you can accomplish more with your free time at the office. This could be done by the following:

- Have your receptionist manage the incoming calls to allow you to return them all at once, as soon as you are available.

- Use a smart phone to view emails and faxed documents, copy or scan with the camera, voice notes or recordings, store common forms or documents for ready preparation or email, etc.
- Group office appointments in a time block to minimize office visits.
- Prepare the client on the phone, prior to an office visit.
- Start your day early, to work without interruptions.
- Use email with clients to maximize efficiency, by minimizing office visits.
- Use video phone as option to an in-person meeting.
- Etc.

Client Database

Create and maintain a client database. A spreadsheet software program is a simple way to create a file or record that is easily manipulated for many uses:

- Client Record
- Prospect File
- Opposing Party Record
- Conflict of Interest Reference
- Mailing List
- Client Account Statement
- Etc.

A database is a valuable tool to help you stay in touch with past and potential clients. Software that has an office suite of programs like a word processor, spreadsheet, image editor, etc., can facilitate a professional follow up system. Mail merging capability will merge your contact information in your spreadsheet into any follow up piece, like a letter, newsletter, flyer, brochure, etc.

Maintain your database with important client and prospect information that may be a good reason to stay in touch. Unlike junk mail that we all receive and throw out, sometimes before reading it, thoughtful and relevant information or message is always welcomed. Welcomed information, message or simply a greeting is very effective in nurturing an attorney-client relationship. Here are examples of important information to keep in your database:

- Name, address, email, phone numbers, work addresses, etc.
- Birthdates (Client & family)
- Graduation (Insurance contracts, investment agreements, leases, trusts, etc.)
- Anniversary (Life insurance policies, trusts, will, etc.)
- Ages of estate beneficiaries
- Date to update a will
- Date when children will be of legal age, affecting guardianship, inheritance, etc.
- Date of incorporation (annual reports)
- Type of business (change of laws that may affect operations)
- Pet's name and type
- Special interests
- Memberships and Associations
- Homeowner or renter (Real estate contracts / leases, insurance contracts)
- Etc.

In addition to the above, you can also stay in touch by sending greetings on holidays, or just to say hello. Another idea is to maintain a newsletter or blog, as discussed in the previous chapter. If the reason to stay in touch is relevant and helpful, it will always be welcomed. Keep track of how many clients or prospects return because you stayed in touch. Remember, that because you stay fresh in their mind, they will be more likely to remember to refer you to others, when the opportunity arises.

Marketing Consistency

Unsteady business flow is the main complaint and challenge of any business. It prevents effective planning and causes unexpected interruptions. It makes a business inefficient with unexpected crisis managements. It is definitely the wrong way to manage a business.

Consistent marketing is a better system. Maintain your advertising efforts, even when you get busy. Fine-tune, change, and eliminate what isn't working. It will keep the phone ringing and keep you busy with steady business.

After a period of six months to a year, you will have an advertising plan that is predictable with the results of new and steady business prospects. You will be able to depend on expected business and will be able to balance other aspects of your life. Your work day will be as full as you like, without inefficiency and waste. However, it does take discipline to maintain consistency with your prospecting. You may want to enlist part time assistance to achieve this.

Marketing consistency also means to continue to find new ways of prospecting for new clients. You want to replace any advertising plan that isn't working with another that does. Never stop prospecting!

As you increase your income, also increase your advertising budget. Look into different ways to advertise that save you more time from prospecting. Again, it is not necessary to reinvent the wheel. Simply pay attention to advertisements from other attorneys. Notice the ones that have been running for a long time. This is a sign that they are getting some results. Newer ads that you don't see any more probably did not produce the expected results.

Advertising in broader media will cost you to run it. However, effective advertising doesn't really cost anything, if it produces paying clients. It just takes an up-front payment to run the ad... Here are some examples of broader reaching advertising:

- Cable TV
- Radio
- Pay Per Click – Internet
- Newspaper

- Mail Outs
- Search Engine - Internet

Surveys

Feedback is very important to the savvy business person. Knowing how well or poorly your work was perceived or experienced by the client is very valuable information. It allows you to correct or enhance the business experience for the client to improve the probability that they will return, as well as refer you to everyone they know. It is not enough for the client to be satisfied with your services; they must be "delighted."

Survey all your clients before, during, and immediately after you complete their case. Their memory of their experience is fresh in their mind. The initial client questionnaire is a survey. Include questions about what they expect. During the work on their case, ask how you are doing. Ask if they are experiencing what they expected. The end survey should be brief, with only three to five questions. The last one is a comment section, where they can expand an answer. Mail it to the client with a thank you letter, and include a stamped return envelope.

Surveying the client for feedback on their experience expresses concern on your part. It may even shape a good response, because the client will perceive that you care and want to make sure they are content with their choice of hiring you. This will leave a big impression, and set you apart from the norm.

Final Word

Congratulations!

I thought it appropriate that we end this book the way we started it. You now have an arsenal of tools to point you in the right direction, towards an adventure of self-fulfillment, independence, and success. You have already crossed the starting line by finishing this book. If needed, go through it again. Use it as a checklist. Use it as a reference. Take good notes to help you plan out a business strategy. I wish you all the best!

The next step is yours...

About the Author

D. Carr is a business consultant and life coach, specializing in professional business start-ups and various self-help topics. He shares his wealth of knowledge and experience, from the many businesses he has successfully owned or managed, through his authored books, recordings, and videos. D. Carr resides in Miami, Florida, U.S.A.

****

Please share your opinion of this book, by writing a review under its listing. Your feedback is greatly appreciated!

You can write the author at:

DCarr0001@gmail.com.

If interested, request an email when new publications become available.

Thank you,

D. Carr